KU-657-504

COMPUTER BASICS

DESIGNING FOR DESKTOP PUBLISHING

How to create clear and effective documents with your DTP program

Diane Hudson

How To Books

2081606

NORTH EAST WORCESTERSHIRE
COLLEGE LIBRARY

070.50285 HUD

Cartoons by Mike Flanagan

British Library Cataloguing in Publication Data
A catalogue record for this book is available from the British Library.

© Copyright 1998 by GST Technology.

First published by How To Books Ltd, 3 Newtec Place,
Magdalen Road, Oxford OX4 1RE, United Kingdom.
Tel: (01865) 793806. Fax: (01865) 248780.
email: info@howtobooks.co.uk
www: http://www.howtobooks.co.uk

First published 1998
Second impression 1999

All rights reserved. No part of this work may be reproduced or stored in an
information retrieval system (other than for purposes of review) without the
express permission of the Publisher in writing.

Note: The material contained in this book is set out in good faith for
general guidance and no liability can be accepted for loss or expense
incurred as a result of relying in particular circumstances on statements made
in this book. The law and regulations may be complex and liable to change,
and readers should check the current position with the relevant authorities
before making personal arrangements.

Cover design Shireen Nathoo Design
Cover image PhotoDisc
Produced for How To Books by Deer Park Productions.
Typeset by PDQ Typesetting, Stoke-on-Trent, Staffs.
Printed and bound by Cromwell Press, Trowbridge, Wiltshire.

DESI NIN3 R ON OP BLIS

208160

A selection of other titles published by How To Books

Arranging Insurance
Buying a House
Buying a Personal Computer
Career Networking
Cash from Your Computer
Communicate at Work
Copyright & Law for Writers
Creating a Website
Creative Writing
Do Your Own Advertising
Do Your Own PR
Doing Business on the Internet
Improving Your Written English
Learning New Job Skills
Learning to Read Music
Making a Wedding Speech

Manage Computers at Work
Managing Budgets & Cash Flows
Managing Your First Computer
Mastering Business English
Planning a Wedding
Publishing a Book
Publishing a Newsletter
Start a Business from Home
Start Word Processing
Using the Internet
Write a Press Release
Writing a Report
Writing for Publication
Writing Reviews

Other titles in preparation

The How To Series now contains more than 200 titles in the following categories:

Business & Management
Computer Basics
General Reference
Jobs & Careers
Living & Working Abroad

Personal Finance
Self-Development
Small Business
Student Handbooks
Successful Writing

Please send for a free copy of the latest catalogue for full details
(see back cover for address).

Contents

Preface

Welcome to the world of desktop publishing. With this guide you will find that creating your documents is easier and more fun than ever before. It is packed with hints, tips and advice about how to make the best of your documents, not to mention a glossary for all those baffling desktop publishing terms. This book will give you the confidence to take your first step towards designing your own documents without the help of a professional designer.

WHAT IS DESKTOP PUBLISHING?

Desktop publishing (DTP) is the combination on the PC of writing skills and design skills that create attractive and readable documents which can be adapted to suit a wide variety of purposes. DTP is to design and publishing what DIY is to building and decorating. With practice we can all become accomplished enthusiasts.

It is only with the recent developments in desktop publishing software that we are able to bring the full power of desktop publishing to your home and business. The emergence of and improvements in DTP have made publishing and high quality presentations readily accessible to the average PC user. In the early years the software and systems required to run it were out of reach for many users, but now they are well within the budget of most businesses and individuals.

Until recently graphic design has been the domain of professional designers, who would take your text and design a suitable page layout for your needs. This is not because designers were the only people who could lay out a document in an attractive way, but because the tools were not available to the average person. The advances in PCs and software have changed that.

In many industries personal computers have merely altered and improved the way we work, but desktop publishing has had an incredible effect on the publishing industry. In the very beginning, publishing your documents was far from easy. Each letter of your text was an individual metal stamp that was positioned in a tray one by one and then inked and pressed onto the paper. This was not only time consuming, but you also needed a professional printer to do it for you.

Although printing and publishing improved and became much easier as new technology was discovered, it was never as straightforward as it is today. Even in more recent times the writer would put the text together and pass it on to a designer, who would organise the page layout and then pass it on to the printer. Now you can create your text and page using the same software and, for budget documents, you can even print them yourself.

Most desktop publishing packages are so simple to use that if you are prepared to experiment you will soon be able to produce professional looking documents. Your PC and DTP software can provide all the tools you need and this book will show you how.

WHO USES DESKTOP PUBLISHING?

Anyone and everyone can have a need for desktop publishing. It could be a cassette or CD sleeve or an internal newsletter for your company – desktop publishing covers a vast range of documents. Desktop publishing is a cost-effective and easy way to produce your documents, but it does not have to be just small-scale. You could produce one or two menus for a café or a whole range of leaflets for your business. Producing your own documents can not only save money and possibly time, but it can also be very rewarding and satisfying. With just a little practice you will notice how much your documents improve. By producing your own documents you maintain full control of their content and appearance.

Effective documents depend not only on good content, but also on appearance. If a document looks appealing your audience is more likely to read it than if it looks dull. Good graphic design can also help you to convey a message or make your document clearer. Just as good design can make a document easier to read so can bad design make it difficult to read. How often have you wanted to read something only to find that the way it appears on the page was off-putting? This book can help you to eliminate these problems.

UNDERSTANDING WHAT THIS BOOK CAN DO FOR YOU

This book will show you that anyone can produce a well designed document if they are willing to take the time to learn a few tricks of the trade. To begin with we will guide you through the basics of designing and creating some of the most popular DTP documents. We will go on to explain some of the principles behind using colour in your documents and then the basics of having your document printed by a professional print bureau. We cannot give you hard and fast rules for designing a document, but we can offer guidelines that will apply in most situations. At the end of the day it all rests on your own judgement and it is this that we will help you shape.

Once your confidence builds you will be able to try different techniques and discover your own style. You will probably be surprised by how much you already know about good design techniques. Just think of the designs that you see around you every day and what you like about them; the ones that stick in your mind are the best designed. Once you decide what it is you like about them you can also use similar designs.

Desktop publishing is a whole learning process that may take some time and probably a great deal of effort, but the results will be worth it. You will not become an accomplished designer overnight, but with continued use you will be able to produce better and more effective documents.

Above all, enjoy what you do and the enjoyment will show through in the documents you produce.

KNOWING HOW TO USE THIS BOOK

This book has been structured in such a way to help you get the most from it and there are a number of ways that you can use it. You can:

- read through the book from cover to cover and absorb as much of the information as possible

- refer to the sections about designing a specific document when you want to produce a similar document

- use **Appendix A: Design advice** as a reference chapter to help you design your documents

- use the **Glossary** to look up any terms you are unsure of

- refer to the index to find information about a specific subject.

However you decide to use this book, you will certainly find it helps you to create your own stylish and effective documents.

Diane Hudson

ACKNOWLEDGEMENTS

I would like to express appreciation to Jeff Fenton, Jason Gardiner, Sarah Hopwood and Mark Leece who all assisted in the production of this book.

1
Looking at Different Types of Document

There is a wide range of documents that you can create using desktop publishing and the type of document you design will depend on what you need it for. Examples of some of the documents you can design and create include:

- newsletters

- brochures

- advertisements

- booklets

- stationery

- posters

- ... and many more.

NEWSLETTERS

A newsletter is a bulletin that is produced periodically and distributed among the members of a group. It could be produced as infrequently as once a year or as often as once a week, depending on the nature and amount of information you have to include. The group it is produced for could be anything from a professional association to a small club. This gives you huge scope for different newsletter designs from the very serious to the seriously fun.

Newsletters can be a quick and inexpensive way to pass on information to your group without requiring too much effort. Once you have decided on the layout for your newsletter use the same one every time, keeping your newsletters consistent, maintaining an identity and cutting down your workload.

BROCHURES

A brochure is a pamphlet or booklet that is designed to offer initial information about your organisation. It can be used as an advertisement for your products or facilities, but would normally lean towards a soft sell approach. A brochure would probably be aimed at people who already have some interest in what you are offering as opposed to trying to get people interested.

ADVERTISEMENTS

Advertisements designed in desktop publishing packages range from small advertisements for magazines and newspapers to large posters that can be pasted around town. Whatever their size, the focus is on making them eye-catching, attractive and clear. How you achieve this will, of course, depend on the nature of the advertisement and where it will be displayed or published. Producing your advertisements yourself is cost-effective and allows you to make last minute changes.

BOOKLETS

Booklets can be used for all different types of documents as they suit a range of styles and sizes. You could use your booklet for a short story or a step-by-step guide to using a piece of machinery. A booklet would normally have a smaller page size than a newsletter and a longer shelf life. It is something that would probably be looked back on and referred to a number of times and your design should reflect this.

STATIONERY

This can be anything from personalised stationery with your name and address at the top to professional business stationery. The range could include letterheads, business cards, postcards and perhaps even envelopes.

POSTERS

Your imagination is the only limit to what posters you can produce. Whether it's a notice for a bedroom door or an advertising poster for a fast food restaurant, desktop publishing gives you the opportunity and capability to create the posters you want.

DECIDING WHAT TYPE OF DOCUMENT YOU NEED

Before you decide on the type of document you need, think about what you want your document to do and how you want to do it. There are a number of considerations:

- What is the **purpose** of your document?

- Who is your **audience**?

- What **information** do you need to include?

- What **image** do you want to project?

- Do you have to conform to a particular **style**?

- How will it be **reproduced** and distributed?

Make all of these decisions before you begin to design your document and decide what type of document will suit your specifications best.

Deciding what type of document you want isn't always easy, but once you have decided exactly what you want to achieve and how you are going to do it, the decision becomes much easier and your choice of document will seem obvious.

2
Designing a Newsletter

Newsletters can be used for a variety of purposes by a variety of people, from a light-hearted school magazine to an internal document for a large company. They are ideal for passing on information in an easily readable format and help to keep people up-to-date with recent news and events. Your newsletter can be produced with varying frequency from weekly to annually. How often it is produced has a direct effect on how much time you can spend designing and creating it. This chapter will show you two examples of well designed newsletters and give you advice about creating your own.

PLANNING THE CONTENTS

The content of your newsletter will, of course, depend on your intended audience. Here are a few suggestions:

- information about your organisation, *eg* new staff, financial reports, new procedures, fund raising events
- letters pages
- advice column
- gossip column
- jokes, cartoons and puzzles
- advertisements.

These are just a few examples of the types of articles and stories you might want to include in your newsletter. Think about your audience and the purpose of your newsletter to help you decide exactly what you need to use.

What makes up a newsletter?

There are a number of components that you will almost always find in a newsletter. It is these components that you need to learn to adapt to suit your style and image:

Masthead – the title of your newsletter. It normally appears at the top of the page and can include the volume number, date and even a brief phrase or motto.

Headlines/headings – the size and style of your headings should vary according to their importance, the largest and most prominent being the most important.

Teasers – a group of short phrases or sentences on the cover of your newsletter that encourage the reader to look inside, *eg* Contents.

Lead-ins – a short paragraph at the beginning of an article or story that would ease the reader in.

Body text – the main text of your articles which will probably be organised into columns.

Pictures – can be photographs, clipart or logos that add something to the article.

When all of these items are positioned together on the page to complement each other, you will have a well designed document.

DESIGNING A COMPANY NEWSLETTER

The following newsletter has been designed as an internal newsletter for the employees of a company. It is intended to pass on information about how well the company is performing and any other useful company information.

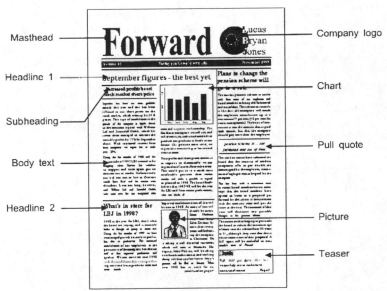

Company logo

The logo on this newsletter front page has been given a very prominent position. There is plenty of white space around the logo to make it stand out easily from the rest of the items on the page.

The company identity is important here and the font style used in the logo has been carried over into the rest of the newsletter.

Masthead

The masthead for the newsletter uses the same font style as the logo, which maintains the company identity and even includes the logo.

The font used is Times New Roman, which is a formal and

traditional font used in many documents and will have a familiar feel for the readers. The text for the title in the masthead has plenty of space around it to make it noticeable. The wide band beneath the title and logo not only separates it from the articles below, but also holds information about the issue number and date of the issue. It also includes a motto which gives you an idea of the attitude of the company that produced the newsletter. Placing the masthead at the top of the page is a traditional approach and adds to the business-like feel of the page.

Headlines and headings

Headline 1 is the most important headline on the page and is, therefore, the largest. The same font as the body text and masthead has been used, but at a point size of 24 and in bold so that it stands out. Headline 2 is smaller than Headline 1, making it clear which is the more important. The point size for this heading has been reduced to 18, which is almost twice the size of the body text. Both headings have been styled in bold to make the contrast between them and the rest of the text even greater.

The subheading is only four points larger than the body text and is styled in bold. The rules (lines) above and below the subheading keep it separate from both the body text and the headline above it. The subheading here is intended as an extension of the main headline.

The line spacing of the headlines has been increased to add white space around them which makes them even more prominent on the page and draws attention to the text. The headlines are left-aligned to make them fit in with the body text and appear neat and tidy; the subheading is centred to increase the contrast.

Body text

The body text of the newsletter is styled in 10 point Times New Roman. Times New Roman was chosen not only because it corresponds with the company logo, but also because it is an easily readable font that is well known and will be familiar to the readers. The text has been justified to keep the columns tidy and well organised and hyphenation has been used to avoid irregular spacing and white rivers appearing.

Pull quote

A pull quote is a short phrase or sentence that has been taken from the main text of the article and used as a design feature on the page to draw attention to the article. These are similar to teasers in that they encourage the readers to read the article.

The rules draw attention to the pull quote while also separating it from the body text. The text is styled in Times New Roman but larger than the body text (12 points) and bold/italic so that it stands out.

The current pension scheme is under attack from many of our employees and board members as being old fashioned and out of date. The scheme as it stands is like this: the company will match the employee's contribution up to a maximum of 7 per cent (10 per cent for senior management). The bone of contention is not the amount that is paid each month, but that the company should pay more than the employee.

pension scheme is ... old fashioned and out of date

The workers' union have informed the board that the majority of modern companies offer to pay double the amount paid by the employee, a maximum of eight per cent to be paid by the company.

Picture

The picture in this article has been used to add some clarity to the information. The company that has produced this newsletter is very large and it is likely that most readers have never met the Sales Director, but at least they now know what he looks like.

The picture is aligned with the left edge of the column and the text wraps itself around it to save space and incorporate the picture into the text.

Chart

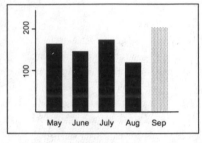

The chart is included in the newsletter to add emphasis to the point being made in the article. Sometimes readers may be drawn to the article because they are interested to know what the chart refers to. It is kept simple so that anyone will be able to understand it. A more complex chart or graph has not been used because the idea is to make the point clear, not baffle the readers.

The graph is aligned to the width of the column to maintain an organised feel to the page and, therefore, give the impression of an organised company.

Teasers

The teaser at the bottom of the page is a bit like a list of contents. It is not used to list the entire contents of the newsletter, but the most interesting articles that would encourage the readers to take a look inside.

> **Inside**
>
> *Profit related pay figures show how we can help you to make more money each month   Page 3*

These are tricks of the trade that you will see on many other newspapers and magazines around you every day.

Page size

The page size used for this newsletter is A4/Letter which is probably the most common for documents of this type. It gives the newsletter a business-like feel which is suited to the company. Using A4/Letter pages also means that you have more space on the page than if you used a smaller page size and is still manageable for people to hold as they read. Using pages that are twice the size of your intended page size and folding them in half to make the pages of the newsletter can make it appear much like a newspaper. Many desktop publishing packages offer you a booklet printing option which will organise the pages so that they print in the correct order according to how you want to put your newsletter together.

DESIGNING A YOUTH GROUP NEWSLETTER

The following newsletter has been designed for a youth group with a large number of members. It is intended to keep them up to date with any recent or forthcoming events. The idea is that the members of the group contribute articles, letters and stories to be included in the newsletter that they then produce themselves.

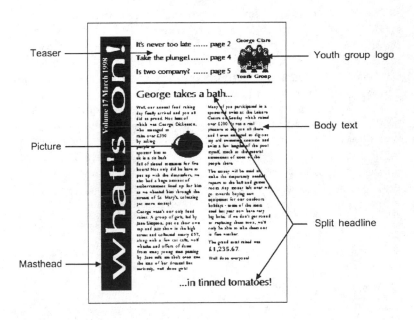

Youth group logo

The logo of the youth group has been positioned so that it is a dominant feature on the page. This is used in a similar way to the logo in the previous newsletter. It gives the newsletter an identity by showing clearly who it is produced by and for.

George Clare

Youth Group

There is a lot of white space around the logo, drawing your eyes towards it and giving an open and relaxed impression. It has also been placed in a very conspicuous position on the page.

Masthead

The masthead for this newsletter has been placed along the left-hand side of the page. This gives the page a less rigid and lighter feel than the previous newsletter.

what's on!
volume 17 March 1998

The font is Autumn, which is a fun and light-hearted font with a friendly and approachable feeling that makes the text seem much more personal. The same font is used in the logo, once again maintaining a consistency and identity throughout. Using reverse text makes the masthead very obvious by creating such a sharp contrast with the rest of the page.

The volume number and release date are also included in the masthead, showing that this is a regularly produced newsletter and that it may be kept and looked back on at a later date. The volume number and date are styled in the same font as the masthead, but are less obvious because they are smaller and almost tucked away in the corner. This makes it clear what is the most important information in the masthead – the newsletter title.

Teaser

The teasers used for this newsletter are vague and cryptic phrases that will whet the readers' appetite so that they are intrigued enough to look inside and found out what they mean.

They are styled in Autumn, size 16 points and bold. This identifies them as separate from the main body text and yet not quite a headline. They are intended to be easily noticed but not to actually draw your attention away from the main article on the page.

Split headline

The headline for the main article on the page is split so that half
appears at the top of the article in the traditional way and the rest is
at the bottom. This gives the article a more personal feeling and
shows an enthusiastic and light-hearted approach to the article. It is
almost as if the headline is meant to be a joke and the second half is
the punchline.

As with the masthead and teasers, the headline is typed in
Autumn, at 22 points and bold so that it is noticeable on the page
and offers a strong contrast to the body text, both in style and size.
The first part of the headline is left-aligned and the bottom half is
right-aligned, implying a continuation in reading and indicating
that they are connected. The headline also stretches across the two
columns of the article, making it obvious that the columns are part
of the same story.

Body text

The body text does not use the same font as the headlines, as in the
previous newsletter, but instead is styled in Toujours (10 points), a
relaxed serif font that is easy to read and has a comfortable feel to it.
The text has been split into two columns and is left-aligned, leaving
a ragged right edge. This gives the impression of welcoming and
gentle text and also creates more space between the columns.

Picture

The picture here has been placed within the text in the left-hand
column and has the text wrapped around it.

did us proud. Not least of which was George Dickinson, who managed to raise over £350 by asking people to sponsor him to sit in a tin bath full of tinned tomatoes for five Centre on Sunday which raised over £200. It was a real pleasure to see you all there and I even managed to dig out my old swimming costume and swim a few lengths of the pool myself, much to the general amusement of most of the people there.

The picture only affects the right-hand edge of the left column and so does not make the text any more difficult to read. Had it affected the left-hand edge of the right column it would have made the text in that column difficult to read.

Rule
The rule between the teasers and the main article separates the two and makes it clear that they are not part of the same story.

Page size
The page size used here is A5/Note, which makes the newsletter seem much more approachable and as if it will be easy and fun to read. A good method for producing this yourself is to fold sheets of A4/Letter in half and then staple them in the middle so that you do not lose the pages.

PLANNING THE LAYOUT

This section details the steps used to lay out and put together the youth group's newsletter.

The page
The first step when you are designing a newsletter is to decide what page size you want, how many columns you will use and what the

page margins should be. The margins and columns will help you position your items more accurately on the page.

The page size is A5/Note with a margin of 1 cm (0.4 inches)

around the whole page. There are five columns with 0.4 cm (0.16 inches) between each. Once the page is prepared you are ready to add the items.

Adding the pieces

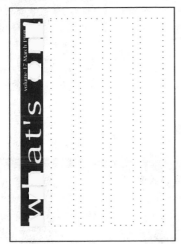

The masthead is added to the page first of all.

The masthead fits the width and height of the first column on the page. Using the column guides as your markers makes it much easier to position the items on the page and size them proportionately. The logo is the next item to be added.

The logo is placed in the top right-hand corner of the right-hand column to make sure that it is aligned properly with the top and right-hand margins. The teaser can now fit in next to the logo.

The text for the teaser tucks in between the masthead and the logo and the rule beneath it defines the area available for the front cover article. These three items are positioned first because they are in the same place for every issue and anything else on the page must fit around them. We are now ready for the article, starting with the split headline.

The frames that hold the headline text are stretched to fit the whole width of the four remaining free columns and aligned with the left-hand edge of the second column and the right-hand edge of the fifth column. The second part of the headline is also aligned with the bottom edge of the columns. The body text is position next.

Each column of text covers two columns on the page, making sure that each column is the same width. If the masthead was the same width as the text columns we would have set the page up with three columns, but as it is the masthead is roughly half the width of the columns for the body text. The final touch is adding the picture to the first column of body text.

This section is by no means a comprehensive guide to laying out your newsletters, but you can see from this how preparing your page setup beforehand will make positioning the pieces much easier.

HINTS AND TIPS FOR NEWSLETTER DESIGN

As with all documents, there are no hard rules for designing your newsletters and those we have shown here are not the only way to do it. Here are a few words of advice for creating your own newsletter.

How many columns?

The number of columns you use is governed by the nature and content of your newsletter (see table below).

No. of columns	Used for...	Advice
One	Serious newsletters, *eg* health news, technical information	• wide columns can be hard to read • use a wide margin, *eg* min 2 cm on an A4/Letter page • use a large font, *eg* 12–14 points on an A4/Letter page • indent headings into the margin to draw attention to them and break up the page
Two	Newsletters with just a few long articles	• allows narrower columns so you can use smaller fonts, *eg* 10 points on an A4/Letter page
Three	Most common format	• more flexibility • can have different size columns • narrower columns are easier to scan through, making the newsletter easier and more relaxed to read • look out for too much hyphenation
Four	Newsletters on larger page sizes than A4/Letter	• can make columns too narrow • look out for hyphenation and white rivers of space • could leave a column for pull quotes or other design features

Developing a style

Most newsletters are produced on a regular basis whether weekly, monthly, quarterly or annually. Your readership is likely to be the

same for each issue and will come to associate the styie of your
newsletters with your organisation. It is important that you build up
a style and use it consistently in all your newsletters.

There are two ways to make sure that you use the same format
and style for each issue:

1. Create your own template for your basic layout, text styles and
    design.

2. Use a previous issue as a basis and just replace the old items
    with your new items.

Being consistent

If you have an item, such as a cartoon, that appears in every issue of
your newsletter, make sure that you put it in the same place every
time. Regular readers should be able to find it without having to
search for it. You should definitely not remove a regular item if you
need to save space – you may find that you receive some complaints
from disappointed and disgruntled readers.

Positioning your headlines carefully

If you have more than one column on your page, be careful that
headlines in different columns do not align with each other as
readers may see them as one line of text.

Separating your columns

When you are using more than one column there is sometimes a
danger that the columns will not be separated clearly. If you think
that your columns seem too close and you do not have the space to
increase the width between them, try using a vertical rule to separate
them. This clearly defines the columns and leads the eyes down
rather than across.

Grabbing the readers' attention

Ideally, the front page of a newsletter should get the readers'
attention and make them pick it up. The next thing they will
probably do is flick through to see what is inside. Make the inside
look appealing by using plenty of pictures and exciting headlines
that will draw them in.

Making the text fit

All too often you will find that your text does not fit into the space that you have allocated to it. Whether it is too long or too short there are ways to combat this.

Too much text
The easiest way to reduce the amount of text by a small amount is by creatively re-writing it so that you say exactly the same thing but with fewer words. If this is not possible you will have to remove some of the text. A good technique for writing articles is to make sure that all of the vital information is in the earlier paragraphs so that, if necessary, you can delete the final paragraph to make the text fit.

Too little text
The most obvious way to increase the amount of text in your article is to go through and add to the sections that are a bit thin. If you still have too much space and not enough text, you could take a sentence or phrase from the article and add it to the article as a pull quote. This not only fills space, but is also decorative.

Looking around you
If you find that inspiration is hard to come by and are not sure what type of layout would suit your newsletter best, take a look at some others produced by different organisations. Look at how the newspapers and magazines are laid out. Take a look at how they have organised their items on the page and the tone and feeling they create by doing this. You will no doubt notice many techniques that you can apply to your organisation's newsletters.

3
Designing a Brochure

Brochures are suitable for a wide range of purposes and organisations. They are most often used to advertise your company, product or organisation and are aimed at a specific audience. Brochures offer a more soft sell approach than the direct advertisement, appealing to an audience that will probably already have some interest in what you are offering. You will find that brochures can be produced in varying formats, the most common being small booklets or leaflets. Booklets are discussed in more detail in Chapter 5, so in this chapter we will assume that brochures are leaflets.

PLANNING THE CONTENTS

The content and layout of your brochure will differ according to its topic and also how you intend to distribute it. Some items that you will want to include are:

- organisation/company name
- product name
- product/company information
- contact details.

These are just the essential items: there will no doubt be many more aspects that you will want to cover. Think about your product/company and decide what are its best features and what would attract your readers to it.

What makes up a brochure?
There are three main aspects of a brochure that you will need to consider carefully when you are designing it. Every component of your brochure will have to be adapted to suit your needs exactly. These are the main parts of a brochure:

Front cover – the front cover of your brochure should announce to the readers what the brochure is about and perhaps encourage them to take a closer look.

Inside pages – this is the section that will have the most impact on your readers. Keep it clear and concise so that your readers can see at a glance what's available.

Back page – the back page is most often used to give contact details, directions or prices that the readers will turn to once you have gained their interest.

Normally brochures will be highly graphic, with lots of pictures and only a minimum of text. What text is included will be kept as short and sweet as possible and get straight to the point. It is something that you hope your readers will keep and refer back to when they are interested. It is not intended to be a hard sell, but rather to persuade people that what you are offering is better than anyone else's.

DESIGNING A BROCHURE TO ADVERTISE A GYM

The following tri-fold brochure has been designed to advertise a gym and is intended to be used for mail shots and to be handed out to people who make any enquiries. It highlights the best features of the gym and also details the special deals they have on offer.

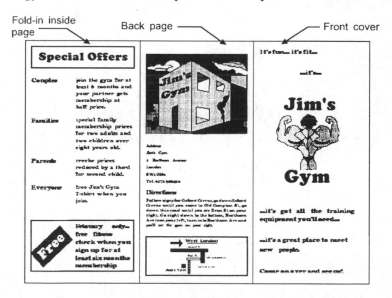

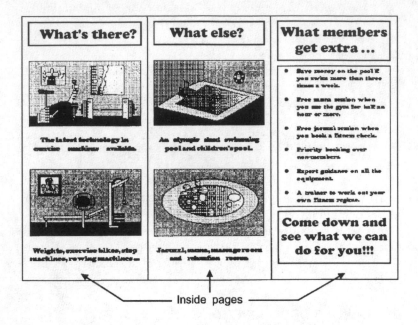

Inside pages

Front cover

The front cover of this brochure is very basic, but quite striking. The logo has been given a very prominent position with plenty of white space around it so that it is clearly emphasised. The most important message here is what the brochure is about. The text on the page is short and to the point and you get the message as soon as you see it. It creates an impact straight away. The text style from the logo has been carried over onto the body text

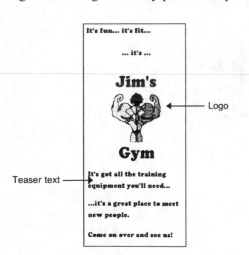

and all other text on the brochure, keeping it consistent and giving it an identity with the gym. The font is Copper Black, which gives the impression of strength and power.

The order that the readers will see the pages in is: the front page, the fold-in inside page, the inside pages, and then the back page. This means that special attention must be paid to the front page and the fold-in inside page to make the reader interested in your topic.

Inside pages

The inside pages of the brochure are designed to draw the readers' attention towards the best features the gym has to offer. The first two pages are mainly pictures with a little text to explain their meaning. The pages that fold inside the brochure have more text and go into more detail about the gym and what it has to offer. Even though there is more text on the fold-in pages, the text is still split into short sentences and bullet points to make sure that the message is clear and immediately obvious.

Copper Black, the font used for the text, is very heavy and should only be used for short pieces of widely spaced text as in this brochure. Too much Copper Black would make the page too dark and more difficult to read.

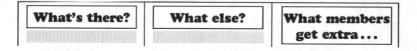

The headings at the top of the pages are boxed to make them more dominant on the page. They are also aligned to the top of each other which helps to lead the readers' eyes across the pages, showing that each page is connected. The rules that separate the pages give the impression of neatness and organisation. They also act as a guide to the readers that they need to work their way down each page and that each is separate.

Back page

The back page of the brochure is probably the last place that the readers will look and should be used to give them the information that they will probably want after reading the main part of the brochure. This could be contact details, directions to your company, prices or perhaps a quick résumé of the main points made in the brochure.

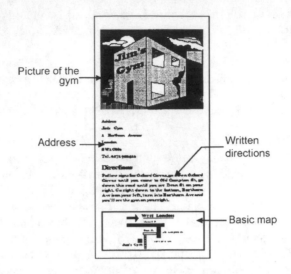

The back page of this brochure is entirely devoted to making it clear how to find the gym. It is not easy to find and every opportunity has been taken to keep directions as simple as possible. The map is basic, showing the street plan from a major location, in this case a main street. The written directions explain how to follow the map, bearing in mind that some people are not very good at reading maps. This way a wide range of people are covered and should be able to find the gym without a problem. There is even a picture of the gym so that they can recognise it when they get there. The address has been given plenty of space to make sure that it is obvious and can be seen clearly. Everything on the back page has been left-aligned to give the impression of uniformity and tidiness. It is more formal than the inside pages, as if it is getting down to the essentials as opposed to the exciting parts.

Once the readers have read the brochure it is unlikely that they will need to read through the main part again. If they do refer back to the brochure it is more likely to be to find out how to get there or how to contact the gym. They do not want to have to search through for the information, but just turn to the back page to find what they want.

Page size

This brochure has been produced on single sheet of A4/Letter, printed on both sides and folded into three. This makes it an ideal size for mailing to potential clients because it will fit into a standard sized envelope.

DESIGNING A BROCHURE DETAILING A STORE'S OFFERS

This brochure has been designed as a point-of-sale brochure for a local supermarket. It is handed out to customers when they leave the store and also delivered directly to the readers' doors via the local newspapers.

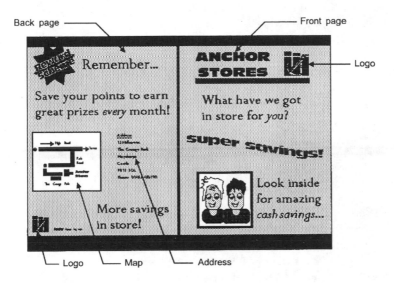

Back page — Front page — Logo

Logo — Map — Address

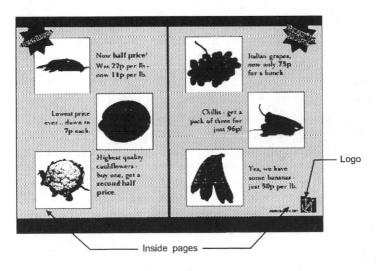

Logo

Inside pages

Front cover

The front cover of the brochure is designed to make the readers want to look inside and 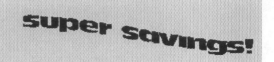 see what there is on offer. One of the main focal points on the page is the text 'super savings!'.

This is the message that the company want to get across to their readers, so it is given a lot of space on the page and an attractive text style to make it stand out. They have been careful to use a text effect that does not make it difficult to read. The font used for the text is the same for the store name at the top of the page.

 This creates a visual link between the store and the phrase 'super savings!' so that the customers will form the same mental link. The logo is positioned dominantly on the page, giving the brochure an immediate company identity and making sure that the customers are instantly aware of what the store is. The rest of the text on the front page is styled in Toujours, which does not stand out too strongly or compete with the 'super savings!'. This text does not jump out at you from the page and needs to be looked at a little more closely. It is hoped that the customers' attention has already been caught when they read this text. The italics are meant to gently emphasise the words, so that the customers do not feel completely overpowered by the hard sell.

Inside pages

The inside pages of this brochure have been laid out in a very neat and organised manner with the same layout on each page so that they look balanced next to each other. The line across the top and bottom of the pages carries over the same design from the front and back pages, giving the brochure consistency. The text is kept short and snappy, just enough to let the customers know what the bargains are. The prices and deals have been emphasised using bold text so that they stand out on the page and the customer does not even have to read through the text to see what is available. The text font is Toujours, as on the front page. Again, this has been used to keep the brochure consistent.

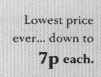

Lowest price ever... down to **7p each.**

Highest quality cauliflowers - buy one, get a **second half price.**

The text is aligned to the same side as the picture it refers to. This makes it clear which product the text refers to, especially as the centre text could be misleading because it has a picture above, to the right and below it.

The line between the pages keeps the two pages separate, making sure that the text for the product at the top of the left-hand page is not thought to refer to the product at the top of the right-hand page.

The starbursts at the top outer edges of the pages are used as eye-catching design effects that stand out on the page.

The font used in these starbursts is Olive Nord MN, the same as that used for the store name and the text effect on the front

page. Once again, this creates a link between the text in these starbursts and the store name.

The logo appears again on these inside pages, making sure that the customer is always aware of the store name.

Back page

The back page concentrates on two topics: the store's reward scheme and directions to the store. Once again, a starburst draws attention to the reward scheme and the same font is used as that for the store name to give it the store's identity. The font used for the other text is Toujours, as in the rest of the brochure.

Although this brochure is used as a point-of-sale brochure for customers to pick up in the store, it is also intended to be distributed in the local newspapers. This is why the map and address have been given so much space on the back page. The map is boxed to draw attention to it. The logo is used yet again to keep up the store identity throughout.

Page size
Each page of the brochure is A5/Note, with two pages printed on each side of an A4/Letter sheet and then folded in half. It has to be reproduced on a glossy paper to make it more appealing to readers and potential customers.

PLANNING THE LAYOUT

This section will explain how the components of the brochure for the gym were put together.

The page
Step one, as always, is to decide on your page size, column guides and margins.

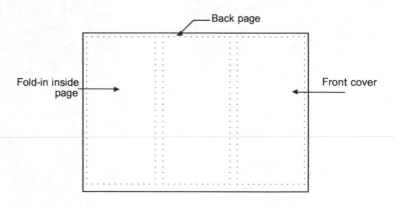

The page used for this brochure is a sheet of A4/Letter paper which is separated into three panels and will be printed on both sides. Three column guides are marked on each page and the space between them is 1cm (0.4 inches). There is a margin of 0.5 cm (0.2 inches) around the whole page.

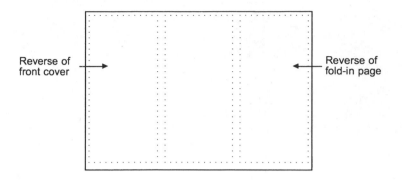

Reverse of
front cover

Reverse of
fold-in page

Adding the pieces

The page layout for this brochure is very simple. Everything is aligned to the three columns for each panel, whether they are centred or left-aligned. First we will concentrate on the inside pages, which have their headings positioned first.

Inside pages

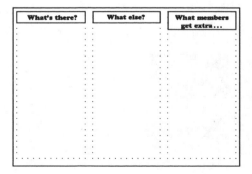

What's there?   What else?   What members
                               get extra...

Each of the frames for the headings is the width of the column and the text is centred in its frame. The frames are aligned to the top of the columns, and therefore, are all aligned to the top of each other. Once the headings are in place the pictures can be added.

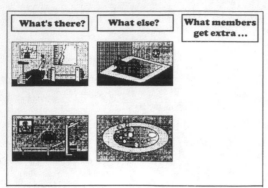

Like everything else on the page, the pictures are the same width as the column, keeping the columns regular and even. What we need to add now is the text.

All of the text, except the bulleted points, is centred to keep the columns balanced and even. The bulleted points cannot be centred because they would look ridiculous. The last remaining items to be added are the rules that separate the columns.

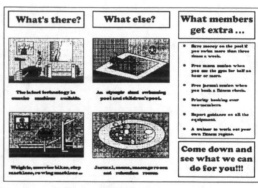

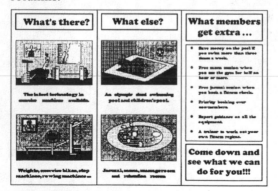

Now we will turn our attention to the front and back pages and the fold-in inside page. The column guides and margins are the same for this page as the inside pages, and in the same way, the pictures and titles are added first.

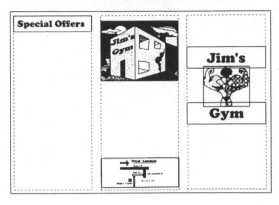

All of these items are centred in frames the same width as the column, except for the strongman picture which is centred in the column. Now the page is ready for the text to be added.

The text is neatly organised into the columns, giving the impression of order and regularity. We are now ready for the final touch, the rules.

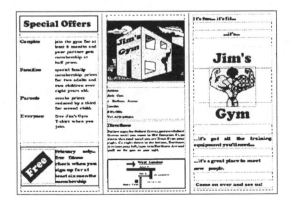

All that remains to be done now is to have the brochure printed, ready to be distributed to potential members.

HINTS AND TIPS FOR BROCHURE DESIGN

These are not the only designs you can use for your brochures. Experiment with different ideas to achieve exactly what you want. Here are a few words of advice to help you create and design your brochure.

Page sizes

You can design your brochures to fit on different sized paper and fold them differently according to the effect you want to create. The following table will give you some idea of what page size to use for your design.

Style	Page size
Two-fold	A4/Letter, A5/Note
Tri-fold	A4/Letter
Four-fold	Legal, Foolscap

Developing a style

The text style you use for your brochure is very important. With such a small document and so little text the visual appeal of the brochure will create an instant impression. Think very carefully about exactly which font, style and size to use so that it suits the tone or feel that you want.

Letting it flow

The content of your brochure should flow naturally from panel to panel. The readers must be able to just browse through easily in a relaxed way. If there is not a natural progression through the panels the brochure will look untidy and unplanned.

Putting it all together

When you are creating your brochure you have a choice of how to do it. You could:

- Design each panel on a separate page and then lay it out in the correct order for printing at a bureau. This is the easiest method for making sure the panels are in the correct order, but it makes it more difficult to align objects on different panels.

- Design the front panels on one sheet of paper and the back panels on another. This makes sure that you have objects positioned correctly with other items, but it is more difficult to order the panels correctly. Fold a blank page in the same way as you would fold your brochure and number the panels. This will help you to work out where each panel will be when the brochure is complete and make your design task easier.

Looking around you

If you are finding it difficult to decide how to design your brochure, take a look at any other brochures you can. You will always find some aspects of brochures that you like and when you piece all this together you will have your perfect brochure.

4
Designing an Advertisement

An advertisement can be anything from a large poster to be displayed around town to a small classified advertisement in the local paper. In this chapter we will concentrate on advertisements to be printed in a magazine or newspaper. An advertisement of this type could be a full page, but as this would be expensive most advertisements are usually relatively small.

PLANNING THE CONTENTS

The way you design your advertisement will depend on its content and purpose, but it will also be affected by your choice of publication. However, there are a few main features that you should always include:

- the topic of your advertisement, *ie* the product or event

- information about your topic that might interest the readers

- a date, time and place

- a call to action, such as a contact number or address.

An advertisement that will be printed in a magazine or newspaper might be on a page with several other advertisements and have to compete for the readers' attention. Your advertisement needs to be as eye-catching as possible so that the readers are drawn to it and it is not merely glanced at and overlooked. If the readers are casually flicking through a newspaper or magazine you will usually only have around two seconds to catch their attention. A full page advertisement must stop the readers in their tracks and make them stop and look at the page. It may not have to compete with another advertisement on the page, but it might have to compete with an interesting article on the facing page.

DESIGNING AN ADVERTISEMENT FOR COMPUTER SOFTWARE

The following advertisement has been designed for a computer software company to advertise their latest piece of desktop publishing software. It is intended to be placed in a magazine that is sold nationwide and will take up a whole page.

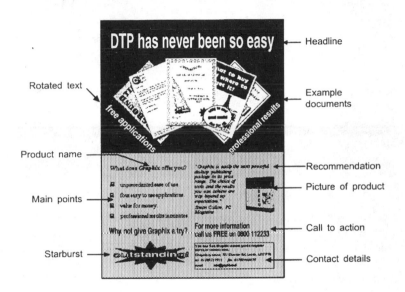

Headline
The headline for this product stands out clearly in the advertisement, not only because it is much larger than the main body text of the advertisement but also because it has plenty of space around it. The font is Sans Narrow which is also used for all the special effect text, such as the rotated text. The white text on the dark background makes the headline stand out clearly on the page and the shadow helps to lift it from the page and grab the readers' attention.

Rotated text
The rotated text is styled in exactly the same way as the headline, but is positioned at an angle of 45 degrees to make it fit with the edge of the end documents. This text effect has been used to make the page appear much more dynamic and give the readers the impression that the product itself is also dynamic.

Example documents

The example documents show what the product can do and act as a focal point on the page.

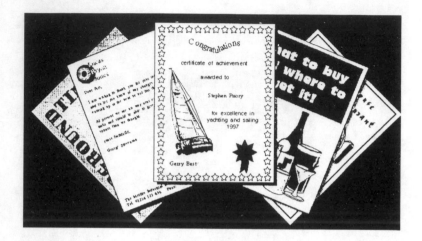

The white pages against the dark background of the page create such a stark contrast that anyone flicking through the magazine would notice the advertisement straight away. The top half of the advertisement gets the readers interested and the bottom half gives them the details.

Product name

Whenever the product name is mentioned in the advertisement it is styled in italics and bold. This emphasises the product name without distracting the readers from the rest of the text. Using italics makes the emphasis less harsh and something the readers would only really notice once they have started reading the text.

The product name is repeated throughout the advertisement, reiterating the topic of the advertisement. The product name is also clear on the picture of the product box.

Picture of product

The picture of the product is useful because the readers might have seen the product in the store already and they will quickly make the connection, making the advertisement more powerful. The advertisers are also hoping that if readers see the product in a store after seeing this advertisement they will be tempted to buy it.

Main points

The key points about the product are listed to draw the readers' attention to them and to make them want to know more about the product. At this stage most readers do not want information about the way the product works and how to use

What does *Graphix* offer you?

- unprecedented ease of use.
- four easy to use applications.
- value for money.
- professional results in minutes.

it, so only the most salient points that are most likely to attract customers are used.

The font used here is Times New Roman (18 points) because it is clear and easy to read. It also offers a contrast to the Sans Narrow used for the text effects. Instead of using bullets to indicate each of the points, small computers have been used. This gives a more fun and approachable feeling and the impression that the software will be fun to use.

Recommendation

Next to the picture of the product we have a quotation from a computer journalist, telling the readers that even the experts like it.

The text is wrapped around the product picture, making it visually clear that the text and the picture are connected. The text is styled in

"Graphix is easily the most powerful desktop publishing package in its price range. The choice of tools and the results you can achieve are way beyond my expectations."
Simon Callow, PC Magazine

Times New Roman (italic, 16 points) to make it slightly different from the main points, but maintaining the connection between the two. It is slightly smaller than the main points because it is considered to be less important.

Starburst

The starburst is used to draw the readers' attention to the advertisement.

It also emphasises the point of the text in the starburst by making it a dominant feature on the bottom half of the page. The same font (Sans Narrow) is used as for the headline and rotated text.

Call to action

The call to action encourages the readers to contact a freephone number that will give them more information about the product.

For more information: call us FREE on 0800 112233

Again Sans Narrow is used for this text. This means that the same font is used for all of the text that is intended to create an impact.

Contact details

The company contact details are styled in italic, the same as the product name. This has been done to differentiate between the main body text of the advertisement and the contact details. The fact that the contact details and the product name are styled in the same way also offers a visual link between the two.

> You can find *Graphix* in most good computer stores, or contact us at:
> *Graphix systems, 231 Charles Rd, Leeds, LD3 PT6*
> tel: 01280 357913   fax: 01280 465839
> *e-mail: sales@graphix.co.uk*

They are positioned at the bottom of the advertisement so that they do not distract the readers from the main body text and are placed in a box to separate them from the rest of the text on the page. The contact details should be clear and easy to find for the readers but should not be forced on them. Readers only need contact details if they are interested in the product.

Page size

This advertisement is designed to be printed on a page size A4 (8.27 x 11.69 inches), the size of the pages in the magazine that will carry it.

DESIGNING AN ADVERTISEMENT FOR A SCHOOL FÊTE

This advertisement has been designed for a school fête and will be printed in the local newspaper. Most people connected to the school will already know about the fête, so the advertisement is aimed more at other people in the town or area.

Title

The title consists of the name of the school and of the event that is being advertised. The name of the school is styled in Mañana (16 points) and the name of the event is styled in Splendid (16 points) – the same font as that used for the body text, but larger. Splendid is a very relaxed and summery font that is well suited to the tone of the

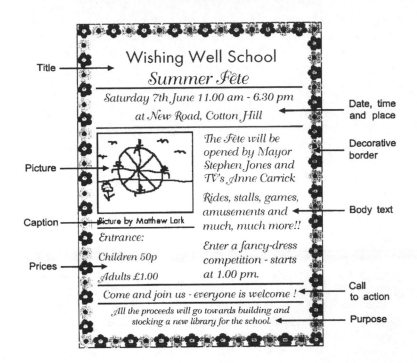

advertisement; Mañana has been used to add a contrast to Splendid so that the name of the school stands out.

The title is centred on the advertisement so that it adds extra space around it. It also makes the advertisement seem more balanced than it would if the text was left- or right-aligned.

Date, time and place

To make the date, time and place of the fête stand out it has been spread across the whole advertisement and also separated from the rest of the text by a rule above and below it. The same font is used as for the name of the event, creating a visual link between the event and the date, time and place.

Picture

The picture has been drawn by one of the children from the school and scanned so that it can be used in the software used to create the advertisement. It depicts the fête and also gives the impression of light-hearted fun. The caption for the picture is styled in Mañana, as used for the name of the school, but this time only in a point size of eight. A caption identifies the artist as a pupil at the school and because it is a local paper it is likely that quite a few people will know him. This makes the advertisement seem more personal and will make it appeal to more readers.

Body text

The body text for the advertisement is styled in Splendid (11 points) and is left-aligned in the right-hand column. The main text has been organised into the right-hand column so that the left-hand column is free for the picture and entry prices. It would be tempting here to have the text justified, but because the text is so large relative to the width of the column it would adjust the spacing too much and make it look untidy.

Prices

This section has been given a great deal of space so that it is clear and easy to see. Although this is not the most important item on the page, it is something that most readers will want to know. The school does not want people turning up on the day claiming that they did not know there was an admission charge. It is styled in the same way as the body text so that it blends in with the rest of the advertisement, but it is set off by the white space around it.

Purpose

The purpose of the fête is the most important point to the school, but the average reader is probably more interested in what will be there and what they can do. People like to know that their money will go to a good cause, but most are not so altruistic as to want to go to an event that will not be fun because it is for a good cause.

All the proceeds will go towards building and stocking a new library for the school.

The text here is styled in exactly the same way as the body text, but spreads across the width of the whole advertisement. A smaller point size (8 points) has been used so that it does not distract from the main body text. It has been placed at the bottom so that it is not mistakenly viewed as part of the main text, but is still visible for those who want to know.

Decorative border

The flowery border is used here for much the same reason as the border on the previous advertisement, to separate it from other advertisements on the page. However, this border is more distinctive than many others and will catch the readers' attention. It also conveys a feeling about the event of fun and summery days.

Call to action

The call to action for this advertisement is an enthusiastic encouragement for people to come along. The borders above and below it make it stand out in the advertisement.

Come and join us - everyone is welcome !

Page size

As with most newspaper advertisements, this is kept to an affordable size: width 7.5cm and height 10 cm (2.95 x 3.94 inches).

PLANNING THE LAYOUT

This section will explain how the advertisement for the school fête was put together.

The page

The first step is to create your page and its column guides.

Once you have decided on your page size you need to decide how many columns you want to work with and what margins you want to have. In this advertisement we have used two columns, a space of 0.3 cm (0.12 inches) between the columns and a margin of 0.6 cm (0.24 inches) around the whole page.

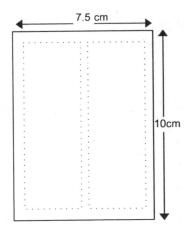

Adding the pieces

Now you are ready to put the items on your page. The first item is a frame the same size as your page that has the decorative border.

The border width is 0.45 cm (0.18 inches) so that there is still a margin between the border and the edge of the columns. Now that you have laid the foundations you can begin to add the text and features. The text that covers the width of both columns is added next.

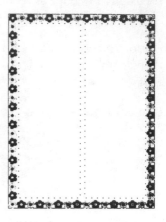

This text has been centred in frames that stretch from the left edge of the left-hand column to the right edge of the right-hand column. This makes sure that they are centred properly on the page. The picture and its caption will be added next, leaving you with the area for the main body text of the advertisement.

Both the picture and the caption have been sized to fit the width of the left-hand column, keeping the appearance neat and organised. The final text can now be added to the advertisement in the space that is left.

Again the text is organised into frames that fit the width of the columns, maintaining the layout. The admission prices have been placed in the left-hand column beneath the picture to keep them separate from the rest of the text. Now the finishing touches are all that are left to be added – the rules that separate different text items.

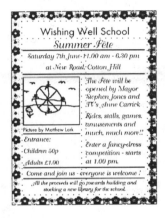

With the rules in place, we are left with the finished advertisement.

HINTS AND TIPS FOR ADVERTISEMENT DESIGN

The most important aspect of a newspaper or magazine advertisement is that it should stand out on the page. The likelihood is that it will be on a page with a number of other advertisements and you want your advertisement to be the dominant one. Here are some tips that will help you design your advertisements.

Adding borders
Depending on the subject of your advertisement, you could add a decorative border which will separate your advertisement from all the other items on the page and draw attention to it. Find a border that suits your subject. If your subject is not suited to a fancy border you can still use a plain border.

If your advertisement is wide, try making the top and bottom edges of the border stronger; a thinner side border will make the advertisement appear taller.

Using white space

If your advertisement is to be on a page that will have several other advertisements at roughly the same size, try leaving a lot of white space both around the whole advertisement and within it. On a cluttered page with lots of text and pictures white space will stand out much more than a border.

Keeping it simple

Above all you want your advertisement to appeal to the readers as soon as they look at it and for them to instantly realise what they are looking at. To make sure that your message is clear, keep the advertisement as simple as possible.

Lots of different pictures and fancy text effects might suit a large poster where you have the space to position them effectively, but in a small advertisement you must be more careful. If space is tight, only include the most powerful headlines or pictures so that the readers will notice them and take a closer look.

The contact details should be clear and easy to see so that the readers do not have to make any effort at all to find them. Put the details in a prominent position, do not tuck them away in a corner. People will not necessarily go to the trouble to find out where you are so you need to make sure that you tell them. It is up to you to make all the essential information readily available.

Short and snappy

Keeping the text short and snappy is the key to making it easy for the readers to register your advertisement. They do not want to search through reams of text to find out what they want to know, you have to make it clear and concise for them. The most effective way of doing this is to use bullet points or a short list of the key points you want to make.

Pictures

Depending on the size of your advertisement you may want to include pictures. This could be just your logo, pictures of your product or anything else that will clarify or emphasise your advertisement's topic. As with all documents that include a company logo you must achieve a balance between having the logo so small that it is not noticeable and so big that it overpowers everything around it. You can draw attention to the pictures in your advertisements by using callouts. These emphasise the prime selling points or important areas and can be recognised instantly. Callouts can also add an educational feel to your pictures.

Size does matter

The size of your advertisement will not only depend on the subject, but also on how much it costs to place it in the newspaper or magazine. A small advertisement can be just as effective as a large one, but remember: the smaller your advertisement, the more restraint you need to not overload it.

Headlines

You will probably find that most headlines for advertisements are centred because this is the most prominent and balanced alignment for such a small document.

A good way to make your headlines stand out clearly on the page is to use inverted text.

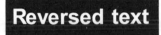

Looking around you

Take a look at the advertisements that your competitors are producing and note down the techniques they use. When you design your advertisement try to do something completely different that will make your advertisement stand out from the others.

5
Designing a Booklet

A booklet can be used for a number of different documents, from a brief manual on using a vacuum cleaner to a large booklet full of short stories. Anyone could have a use for a booklet, whether it be a large company or an individual.

PLANNING THE CONTENTS

Well, basically, absolutely anything could go into a booklet. It all depends on what your booklet is for. It could have a high text content, a high graphical content or could be relatively balanced. With other types of documents you can be sure that certain items will be included, but because booklets can be used for so many different purposes we cannot assume anything about its content.

This chapter will show you two different types of booklet to give you some idea of what booklets can be used for and how they can be laid out on the page and put together.

DESIGNING A CD COVER

The booklet on page 55 has been designed as a CD cover and contains information about what is on the CD and the group who made it. To save time and space we will look at the cover and one of the inside pages.

Group name
The name of the group has been included on both the cover and the inside page of this CD sleeve. This maintains an identity with the group throughout the booklet.

The text has been styled in the same font as the body text of the booklet, but much larger and in outline style. The letter spacing is so tight that some of the letters even overlap each other. This gives the text a modern and fashionable feel. The text has been positioned so close to the edge of the page that it slightly overlaps the border.

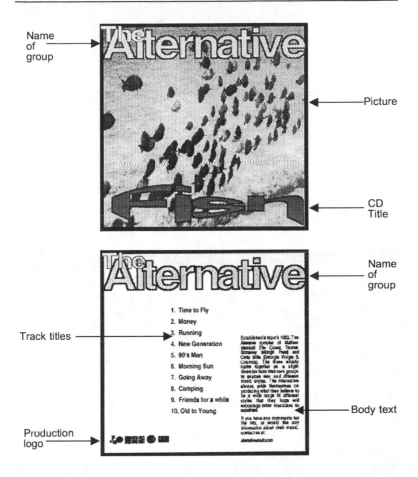

Name of group

Picture

CD Title

Name of group

Track titles

Body text

Production logo

CD title

The CD title has been styled using the same font and outline style as the group name, but has been given a special text effect to make it appear in the shape of a fish.

This creates a link between the title, the style and the picture and again gives it a modern feel.

Picture

The picture on the cover fills the whole page and is used as a background for the text. For once the picture is not the focal point, the title of the CD is the most dominant feature on the page. It is almost as if the picture is intended to evoke a feeling.

Track titles

The list of track titles is positioned in the middle of the page, with a wide space on its left-hand side. This draws the readers' eyes towards it and makes it a clear focal point on the page. The same font is used as for the group name and CD title, maintaining the relationship between all three. The line spacing for the track titles is wide, making it easy to pick out one particular track.

Body text

The body text is tucked away in the corner in much the same way as the picture on the front cover. The font (Sans Narrow, the same as for all the other text on the CD cover) and tight line spacing again give the impression of fitting a lot into a small space.

Production logo

There is a column of white space on the left-hand side of every page, for the same reason as the white space is left on the front cover. The production logo has been placed at the bottom of this column to make it obvious, but it has not been produced so large that it becomes obtrusive and distracts from anything else on the page.

Page size

The page size for this booklet is determined by the size of the CD case, 12 cm by 12 cm (4.73 by 4.73 inches). This is one occasion where you cannot adjust the size.

DESIGNING A GARDEN CENTRE CATALOGUE

The booklet on page 57 has been produced for a garden centre as a catalogue of their products and to give the customers gardening information. It will be handed out to people when they come to the garden centre.

Logo

The logo for the garden centre consists of the name of the centre styled with a special text effect to make the first line arched.

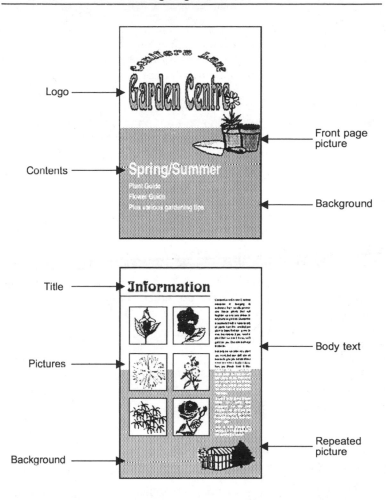

This is the same logo that is used on their signs, carrier bags and work clothes. The font used is Arnold Bocklin, which looks a little like vines or plant roots, to underline the association with plants. There is a lot of space around the logo, making it the most dominant feature on the page.

Front page picture
The picture on the front page overlaps the text on the logo, visually combining the plant and the text. This gives the text more meaning and highlights what the catalogue is about.

Background
The background appears on every page of the catalogue, maintaining a consistency throughout. This can be green which will not only add a design feature to the page, but also strengthen the gardening link.

Contents
The contents of the booklet are printed on the front page to give the readers some idea of what is in it. The catalogue will be available in-store and customers will not take it if they do not know what it is. The text is white because it will stand out against the green background more clearly than black text. The white text on the green background also balances the green logo text on the white background.

Title
The titles for the sections of the catalogue are styled in the same font as the garden centre logo. This carries the same image throughout the booklet, making it seem consistent and also giving it a closer identity with the garden centre.

Information

It is placed at the top of the page and aligned to the left-hand side, keeping the page neat and tidy. The underscore beneath it helps to keep it separate from the text on the page and also draws attention to it. The title appears in this position on every page.

Body text
This is placed in a column on the right-hand side of the page and is styled in Sans Narrow, the same font used for the contents on the front page. This sticks to the golden rule that you should use no more than **two fonts** in a single document.

The text is justified to keep the column tidy, but the words have not been hyphenated. This means that special attention has been paid to make sure that the word and letter spacing are not stretched too much to make the words fit. The text that flows onto the background has been coloured white. This has been done to make it the same as the contents text on the front page and make it easier to read on the green background.

Repeated picture

The picture of the greenhouse and trees appears in the same position on every page. This has been done partly to add a design feature that follows throughout the whole catalogue and partly to emphasise the topic.

Page size

The page size, A5/Note, has been used because it is big enough to include all the information you need on a page and small enough to be easily readable and appeal to the readers. A booklet this size is also handy to fit into a carrier bag as the customers leave the garden centre.

PLANNING THE LAYOUT

This section will show you how the booklet for the garden centre was laid out and put together.

The page

The first thing you need to do is create your page and column guides which will help you position your items on the page.

The page size is A5/Note with a margin of 1 cm (0.4 inches) all the way round. Three column guides have been set up with a width of 0.5 cm (0.2 inches) between each. This layout applies to every page in the booklet.

Adding the pieces

Now that the page is ready, we can add all the items that will make up our booklet. As we have shown you two pages of the booklet in this chapter we will show you how each was put together, starting with the cover.

The first items to add are the background frames, although the colour will not be applied to the lower background until the end. The colour of the frame would obscure the column guides and make it difficult to position the other items.

The upper frame creates a thin border around the page edge and the lower frame is the green background frame. Now we can add the garden centre logo to the page.

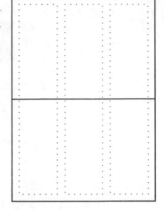

The logo comprises two different frames aligned to the left edge of the left-hand column, making sure that they are lined up with each other properly. Now that the logo is in place we are ready for the picture.

This picture is aligned with the right-hand edge of the page to make sure that it does not obscure the logo and also so that it does not become the main focal point. The contents text is the last item to be added to the front cover.

You cannot see the text at the moment because it is coloured white, but once the background frame has been coloured green it will all become clear. You can see that the frames to the text have been aligned to the left edge of the left-hand column in the same way as the logo. All that is left for the cover is to add the colour to the background.

The inside pages have the same background layout as the cover page. After the background frames have been placed on the page we can add the title.

The title text is aligned to the left edge of the left-hand frame in the same way as the logo and contents text. The top edge of the frame is aligned to the top edge of the column guide. The rule starts from the left edge of the page and covers the left and middle columns. The title for every page will appear in this position. The picture that is repeated on every page is added next.

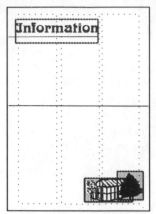

This is positioned in the bottom right-hand corner of each page and extends slightly into the margin. This is added before any other pictures or text because it will appear on every page and the other items must be placed around it. The pictures of plants are then added.

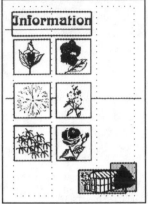

These pictures are aligned with the left and middle columns, keeping them looking organised and tidy. On the other pages of the booklet where the plants are listed with their prices and gardening advice the pictures are in the left-hand column

and the text referring to them stretches over the middle and right-hand columns. The text for this page is an introductory text and is added last.

The text is aligned with the right-hand column, maintaining the organised layout started with the pictures. The final touch is adding the colour to the lower background frame.

Both pages that we have shown you are now complete and with the guidelines shown here, the remaining pages are easy to lay out.

HINTS AND TIPS FOR BOOKLET DESIGN

There are a number of practical issues to be considered before you actually begin to design and create the content of your booklet. What size do you want the booklet to be? How do you want to bind it? And, as ever, how are you intending to have it reproduced?

Size

The size of your booklet not only refers to the size of the pages, but also to how many pages it has. Booklets with a small page size are often more accessible and friendly looking, so readers are more inclined to pick them up and have a look through. Booklets with a larger page size are well suited to formal documents that will probably hold a lot of information.

A booklet with very few pages may look as though it has very little of interest in it. To counter this, try using a smaller page size so that you can increase the number of pages and make your booklet appear more substantial. If on the other hand your booklet is very thick, use a larger page size to spread the content over fewer pages and make it look more appealing.

Binding your booklet

How you bind your booklet depends on whether you intend to have your pages folded in half to make two booklet pages or individual sheets to make each booklet page.

Folded sheets

The options for binding your booklet are:

- Fold the sheets and **staple** them in the middle (also known as saddle-stitched) – you may be able to do this yourself, but you will find that most professional binding bureaux will either be able to do this for you or may be able to recommend someone who can.

- Fold the sheets and **sew** them either by hand or with a machine using a heavy thread. This can be done yourself and will save on money if you have the time to do it.

- Fold the sheets, **punch holes** at the fold and bind them with a brightly coloured ribbon or yarn. Once again this will save time and can be very effective for light-hearted booklets.

Single sheets

The options for binding your booklet are:

- **Punch holes** in the sheets and put them in a binder. The booklet will be hard-wearing and you can replace pages with more up-to-date information or insert new information at the relevant place. This is ideal for long-term booklets where information may need to be regularly changed or added to.

- **Wire-o** or **spiral binding**, which will allow the pages to lie flat when opened and would suit a booklet such as a cookbook or instruction guide. For extra effect you can use colour bindings.

- **Comb binding**, which is similar to spiral binding but normally works out cheaper and you can buy machines so that you can do it yourself. The only down side to comb binding is that the pages can sometimes get caught up in the bindings.

- **Velo binding**, which is plastic strips that are placed on the outer edge of the binding area and connected by plastic pins that go through the sheets of paper. This gives the booklet a quite formal appearance.

- **Tape binding**, which is a special tape placed over the edge of the book and heated to make the inside pages stick to it. This type of binding will lie flat and looks serious although you must be careful to leave a large binding margin to make sure everything on the page is visible.

Think about what you are designing your booklet for. If it is something that will be used a lot it will need to be sturdy enough for repeated use.

Trial run

Make up a sample booklet with the binding that you intend to use. This will give you a good idea of whether the binding is suitable and what width margins to allow for the space the binding uses.

How the pages look

When you are designing a booklet you must pay attention to the way facing pages look next to each other. Do you want to use the same layout or mirror it? Design features on the page can lead you across the pages and thus through the booklet. Your pages must look well balanced when they are seen together.

Looking around you

Take a look at booklets similar to the one you want to produce. Look at how they are laid out, the bindings, page size and even the fonts used. All of this will give you a clearer idea of how you should produce your own.

6
Designing Business Stationery

You can have your stationery designed by a professional designer, but if you know what image you want to project and are willing to spend some time trying out different ideas you can easily create your own. You can create stationery for personal use, as well as business, using the principles described in this chapter.

EXAMINING DIFFERENT TYPES OF STATIONERY

There are three pieces of stationery that you are most likely to need:

- letterheads
- business cards
- envelopes.

Your business stationery should be designed to convey a message about your organisation at first glance. Your stationery may go before you and your prospective customers/clients/associates will form an opinion of you from this.

Assessing the information needed

Each piece of business stationery will require slightly different information, but they will all need the following:

- business name
- logo
- address
- telephone/fax numbers, e-mail/web address.

Business cards will also include a user's name and job title.

The way each of these items is styled will be carried over onto each piece of stationery. This creates a consistent look that helps you give the impression that you are a large organisation and establish confidence in your customers.

DESIGNING BUSINESS STATIONERY FOR A PRE-SCHOOL GROUP

The business stationery below has been designed for a pre-school group.

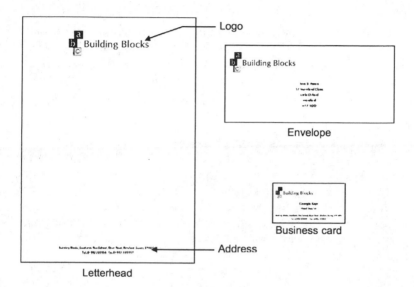

Logo

Envelope

Business card

Letterhead

Address

Logo

In all three pieces of stationery the logo is placed at the top of the page. On the letterhead it is positioned in the centre of the page, whereas on the envelope and business card it is in the left-hand corner.

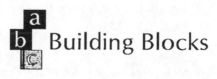

Trying the logo in the left-hand corner of the letterhead made the page appear unbalanced because of the large space between the logo and the address.

To centre the logo on the envelope would reduce the space available for the address of the recipient. Centring the logo on the business card would reduce the amount of space around the person's name, which should be the focal point.

The font used in the logo is Autumn, which is also used for all the other text, maintaining a consistency and company identity.

Address

The address on all of the stationery is positioned at the bottom centre of the page. This is a modern approach not only to the positioning of the address but also for the layout of text for the address.

Building Blocks, Studlands Rise School, Dean Road, Amsford, Surrey SY4 6KN
Tel: 01992 23954 Fax: 01992 235957

Instead of using the traditional approach of a new line for each line of the address, the whole address has been written on one line. This takes up less space on the page and also acts as a sort of rule to mark the end of the page. The same font is used for the address as for the logo, this helps to associate the two both visually and mentally.

The rest of the text

The remaining text used on the business stationery is the customer's address on the envelope and the person's name and job title on the business card. This text is styled in Autumn, like the logo and the address, to maintain consistency.

The address on the envelope is centred to make the envelope appear balanced. The centred text also gives the impression of friendliness and seems relaxed, thus creating an impression of the company even before the letter has been opened.

The name and job title on the business card have been given a lot of white space around them to make them stand out on the page. The name of the person is styled in a larger size and bold to make it the most prominent item on the card.

DESIGNING BUSINESS STATIONERY FOR AN INTERIOR DESIGN COMPANY

The business stationery on page 69 has been designed for a company of interior designers, whose image is all-important.

Logo

The logo on all three pieces of stationery is positioned in the top left-hand corner. This gives the stationery series a consistency of design feature, both by using the logo on all three pieces and also by positioning the logo in the same place each time.

The font for the text in the logo is carried over and used for all the text in the stationery. The font is Mañana, which has a very modern and organised

**OKA
MAN**

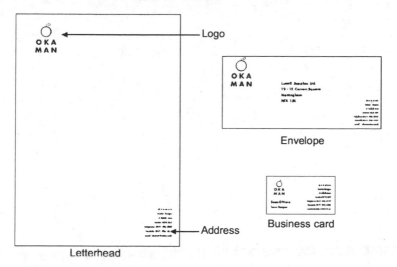

Logo

Envelope

Business card

Address

Letterhead

feel. This corresponds with the image the company is trying to create and conveys a message at first glance.

Address

Just as the logo is in the same place for each piece of stationery, so is the address, again maintaining the design throughout.

OKAMANI
Interior Designs
3 Suffolk Lane
London EC1E 0AT
Telephone 0171 290 2277
Facsimile 0171 296 4422
e-mail okamani.info@.co.uk

The address in the bottom right-hand corner makes the pages appear well balanced and leaves plenty of space in the centre of the page for the letter or for the recipient's address on the envelope. The font used is the same as for the logo, creating an obvious visual link between the two. The text is right-aligned to fit neatly into the corner.

The rest of the text

The recipient's address on the envelope is again in the same font as the address and logo text to keep up the company identity, but at a larger size (14 points) and in bold to make sure it is the dominant text on the envelope. It is left-aligned and centred on the envelope, giving a more serious and business-like impression.

The person's name and job title are left-aligned on the business card and have plenty of space around them to make them stand out clearly. The person's name is larger and bold to make sure that it is the focal point on the card.

Page size

Both sets of business stationery use the same page sizes. The page size for the letterhead is A4/Letter as this is the standard size for business correspondence. The envelope is the standard size (DL) which is roughly a third of the size of A4/Letter. The business card is 9 cm by 5 cm (3.55 by 2 inches) which is similar in size to a credit card, making it easy to carry around because it fits conveniently into a wallet or organiser.

PLANNING THE LAYOUT

This section will show you how the business stationery for the interior design company was put together and laid out on the page. By looking through this you will see how simple it is to produce well designed and effective stationery.

The letterhead

The letterhead is arguably the most important part of your business stationery. It will be seen with every piece of correspondence you send and the same design will be carried over onto your other stationery. The page layout for stationery is much more basic than many other documents you might create.

The page size used for the letterhead is A4/Letter, with a margin of 1.5 cm (0.6 inches) at the top and 1cm (0.4 inches) at the remaining three edges, and just one column. The letterhead is so straightforward that all that remains to be done is add the logo and address.

Now that the design for the stationery is established you can apply it to your envelopes and business cards.

Envelope

Firstly, you need to decide on your page size, margins and column guides.

The envelope is 22 cm by 11 cm (8.63 by 4.25 inches), known as DL. It has a margin of 0.75 cm (0.3 inches) around each edge and, just as with the letterhead, one column.

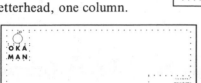

The logo and address can be put in place in the same way as on the letterhead.

The logo is aligned with the top and left-hand edges of the column guide and the address is aligned with the bottom and right-hand edges, just as in the letterhead. All that remains for the envelope is to add the recipient's address.

The text is aligned with the centre of the page so that it is obviously the recipient's address and not the company's address. We are now ready to carry this design over onto the business card.

Business card

You will know by now that the first thing we need to do is decide on the page size, margins and column guides.

The page size for the business card is 9 cm by 5 cm (3.55 by 2 inches) with a margin of 0.5 cm (0.2 inches) all around and one column guide. Again we can add the logo and address in exactly the same way as for the letterhead and envelope.

As with the other pieces of stationery, the logo is placed in the top left-hand corner and the address in the bottom right-hand corner. The name and job title are added below the logo.

This text is aligned with the bottom and left-hand edges of the column guide. Now that you know how easy it is to transfer your design onto a range of stationery you can go on to create your own.

HINTS AND TIPS FOR BUSINESS STATIONERY DESIGN

This section offers general advice about how to design your series of business stationery.

Letterheads

As with all documents, be careful not to let the logo overpower the page, but be sure to make it a dominant feature. Your company name may be incorporated in the logo or you may want to find a way to build the company name around it.

Above all you need to leave enough space for your actual letter. If your letterhead is too dominant and takes up a lot of space it will distract the readers' attention away from the actual letter. The content of the letter is the important information; the letterhead should convey information about the company and give the letter an identity so the readers can tell who it is from immediately.

Think carefully about where you place your information on the page. If you are intending to use **window envelopes** make sure that you leave space to type the person's address so that when the letter is folded and put in the envelope the address appears in the window.

There are a number of different ways to keep the letterhead information separate from the main letter text. Try enclosing the letter area in a box – the style of the borders you use will depend on the style of your letterhead. A simple rule across the page is equally effective.

Your address does not necessarily need to be positioned at the top of the page. In recent years more and more addresses are being printed across the bottom of the page.

The main idea is to keep the letterhead uncomplicated and convey the right impression of your organisation.

Envelopes

Envelopes are the first thing your customer/client will see of your correspondence and thus play a very important role in establishing a good first impression.

You will need to carry over the design used in your other stationery to maintain consistency. The font used for the text on the envelopes should be the same as that used for the name and position on the business cards.

Business cards

Before you begin to design your business card, decide what size you want it to be. Roughly the same size as a credit card is the standard, because they are easy to store in wallets or organisers. You need to include a lot of information in a very small space and so it needs to be as simple as possible. The style you used for your letterheads should be carried over onto your business cards to maintain your oganisation's identity. This means not only the design itself but the colours and fonts should also be used for the name and job title.

When you are designing your business cards remember to leave plenty of space for the name and job title. This should be quite separate from the main design and the most conspicuous item on the card. It must be obvious who you are and what you do. The name should be slightly more prominent than the job title.

Looking around you

Take a look at other organisations' stationery and try to do something a little bit different so that yours stands out from the rest. You will find different layouts and designs that you like. You can then decide which will suit your organisation best and adapt these designs to suit you.

7
Checking for Mistakes

After your document is complete take a good look at it as objectively as possible and try to decide if there is anything you need to change. If you cannot be objective, ask a friend or colleague to take a look for you and give you their honest opinion.

LOOKING AT COMMON PROBLEMS

When you take a look at your finished document you will probably find that there are a number of things you are not happy with. This chapter points out some of the most common problems and offers some advice about how to fix them.

Too much on the page

Limit the number of items on your page to around five (depending on the size of your page). An item can be a paragraph of text or a picture, as long as it provides a focal point on the page.

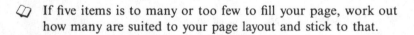 If five items is to many or too few to fill your page, work out how many are suited to your page layout and stick to that.

The page is too dark

If your page is too dark the text will be difficult to read and the items on the page will not be clear. To lighten the page, try any of the following:

- increase the width of the margins

- increase the line spacing

- increase the word spacing (remember, be careful)

- increase the amount of space around the items on the page

- reduce the amount of bold text you have used

- reduce the amount of underlined text

- use a more open font.

Too many fonts

If you use too many fonts in your document it will look untidy and disorganised. Only use two different fonts per document, one serif font and one sans serif font. In general, sans serif fonts are best suited to headlines and titles and serif fonts are most suitable for body text.

📖 Never use two serif fonts or sans serif fonts in the same document unless you have a specific reason.

White rivers in your text

White rivers of space will sometimes appear in your text if you are using justified text and have not allowed for hyphenation. To solve this, do one of the following:

- change the text alignment to left-aligned

- turn on hyphenation

- re-write the text to make it fit

- as a last resort, alter the word spacing but be *very* careful about how it looks on the page.

A word on a line on its own

A word that appears on a line by itself at the end of a paragraph is called a *widow*, *eg*:

> The quick brown fox
> jumped over the lazy
> dog.

To counter this problem:

- change the length of the lines

- re-write the text

- change the word spacing, but be *very* careful.

The last line of a paragraph starts the next column or page

The last line of a paragraph that goes over onto the next column or page is called an *orphan*, *eg*:

The quick brown fox jumped over the   hill with Jack and Jill.
lazy dog just after the dish ran away
with the spoon. Then the little dog was
laughing so much that he fell down the

To correct this do one of the following:

- change the length of the lines

- move a picture to make more space in the column or page where the paragraph begins

- re-write the text

- insert a column or page break at the beginning of the paragraph (or other convenient position) so that the whole paragraph is moved onto the next column or page

- adjust the word spacing, but be *very* careful.

Too much hyphenation

If you have allowed automatic hyphenation you may find that too many words have been hyphenated, making the text look untidy and difficult to read. Correct this by:

- going through the text and manually hyphenating the words you want

- turning off the hyphenation

- re-writing pieces of the text.

The page is too fussy

When you are still relatively new to desktop publishing you can easily get carried away with the design effects your DTP package can produce. While your software might offer you an array of eye-catching and dynamic design techniques, they will not necessarily be suited to your document. Over-the-top designs can often be more distracting than attractive, so remember the following:

- If you have used special design styles, tone them down.

- The best motto to keep in mind is *keep it simple, keep it clear*.

If your problem has not been covered in this chapter, decide exactly what your problem is. Very often, discovering your problem is half the battle to solving it.

8
Understanding Colour and Commercial Printing

If you have never developed a document to be printed professionally you may, initially, find the prospect daunting. This chapter will help you decide what type of colour to use and how to handle your initial dealings with the printing bureau.

LOOKING AT COLOUR

The two different types of colour that you can use in your documents are spot colour and process colour.

Spot colour

When you use spot colours in your document each colour is mixed separately before being applied to the page. This is the best colour type to use if you have a specific colour that you must use, *eg* a company colour.

Process colour

Documents printed using process colours are sometimes referred to as **full colour** documents. This is because process colours are made up from a combination of Cyan, Magenta, Yellow and Black (CMYK) which can be used to create most colours.

Which type of colour should I use?

The flow chart on page 79 will help you decide which type of colour you should use.

Spot colours can normally be printed at a higher resolution, which makes the output sharper and clearer. However, printing spot colours can take longer because the colours must be mixed first. Spot colours are most often used for documents that need to be reproduced in high volume or if you must use a company colour or logo.

Process colours are normally used when the document uses more than three colours. They are not always as consistent as spot colours

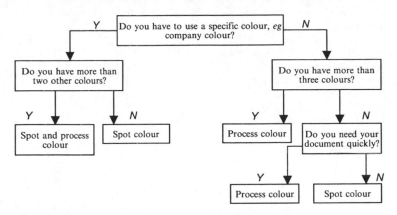

as the colours are combined on each page to make the colour you want and may differ slightly. Process colours should be used for documents with colour photos or brightly coloured pictures and documents that will be reproduced in small numbers or are only a single page.

In certain circumstances you may need to combine both spot and process colours in your document, perhaps for a full colour document with a company logo. This can be done, but be aware that it may cost more. Your printer will be able to advise you of the most cost-effective way to print your document.

DECIDING WHICH METHOD OF PRINTING YOU NEED

Once you have decided what colours, the type of paper and the size of the paper you are going to use, you need to decide what method of printing you will need. This section and the table on page 80 will help you decide which option is best for your needs.

Desktop printing
Desktop printing means printing your document on your own desktop or network printer. It has a number of advantages, most of all that it is close at hand and offers instant results.

Black and white professional printing
You may be able to produce high resolution (600 dpi) copies on your desktop printer, but find that your printer cannot take the type or size of paper that you need or you do not have the time to print the number of copies you need. This is when using a professional printer to reproduce your documents can save you time and effort.

Method	Best for...	Comments
Desktop printing	• small number of copies • masters for the printers • proofing and experimenting • using pre-printed paper	• low cost • average quality (depending on printer and paper) • quick and easy
Black and white professional printing	• printing on larger paper (A3/11″ x 17″ or above) • printing on both sides of the paper • using special paper • documents that need to be bound, trimmed • menus, booklets	• very good quality • relatively quick returns (24 hours) • good for high volume reproduction • more expensive than desktop printing
Full colour printing	• documents with colour photos • documents that don't need heavy paper • paper up to A3/11″ x 17″ • one page documents	• good quality • reasonably quick returns (24 hours) • expensive
Spot colour printing	• high volume • documents that use a company colour • organisation newsletters • black and white newsletters with one other colour	• very high quality • more difficult to set up initially • the more you print, the less it costs per copy • slower returns

Full colour printing

Otherwise known as process colour printing, this can be especially useful if your document has colour photos or is multi-coloured. Using a professional printer for this means that you can be more sure of the colour quality.

Spot colour printing

Spot colour printing is a more complicated printing process, but the results are definitely worth the effort if your document is an important official document. Although spot colour documents can take a lot longer to have printed, the results will be perfect and the colours exactly what you need.

Cost

The cost of having your document printed professionally will depend largely on the quantities you want reproduced. The setup costs may seem steep, but if you are having a large quantity reproduced you will notice that the cost per copy reduces the more copies you have.

DEALING WITH THE PRINTER

You need to talk to your printer when you have an idea of the document you want to create and before you actually begin to design it. You will need to discuss your ideas with the printer and check if they are viable. You will need to tell the printer:

- your budget
- how many copies you want
- if you intend to use colour
- how many colours/what type of colours you will use
- the number and size of pages
- what fonts you want to use
- the quality you want your document to be, *eg* the type of paper you want
- the software you intend to use.

The printer will then be able to tell you if this is all possible and advise you of any alternatives if it is not possible.

KNOWING WHAT TO ASK THE PRINTER

You will need to find out if your printer has any special requirements for instructions or how you should give him the document to be printed. Here are a few questions you should ask the printer:

- What format does he want the document in? Camera ready copy (printed on your desktop printer) or on disk?
- Will he produce a draft to check through? Mistakes can be expensive to rectify later.

- If he wants the document on disk, what printer driver should you use?

- What colour matching system does he use? (*eg* Pantone).

- If you are printing more than one colour, do you need to specify an order they should be printed in?

- Can he suggest a way to reduce costs without reducing quality?

Your printer will have a better idea of how a document should be printed and if there is anything you want to know, he is the one to ask. You will probably find that he has a number of suggestions for making your printing task more effective.

UNDERSTANDING COMMON PRINTING TERMS

When you are dealing with the printer you will no doubt come across a number of terms that you do not understand. Here are a few to help you get started.

Knocking out and overprinting

When you create a multicolour document, it is likely that at some point the colours will overlap. Most desktop publishing packages will then give you the option of knocking out the colour underneath or overprinting it.

> **Knocking out** – the bottom colour does not print on the page where the top colour would overlap it and the top colour is printed directly onto the page.

> **Overlapping** – the top colour prints directly on top of the bottom colour.

Overlapping colours can cause the colours to blend together, resulting in the wrong colour and also means that more ink is printed onto the page than you need.

As a rule, you should normally overprint the black text. This means that the text prints neatly and no space will occur if the printing is misaligned.

Trapping

In multicoloured documents the printer must print each colour separately onto the page. Occasionally the press is not aligned properly and one or more layers may print slightly out of place. If you are printing knock-out colours, you may have a white space where the colour has not printed. If you are overprinting colours, the colours will not blend fully to the edges. With process colours, misaligned printing can cause the object to have different coloured edges as the colours will not be mixed together in the right place.

Trapping is a method that has been designed to slightly overlap adjacent colours in order to avoid any noticeable misalignment. Some desktop publishing packages will let you set these properties yourself, but if not, there are pre-press services available that will do it for you or your printer may do it for you before he prints the document.

Colour separations

When you are printing a colour document each colour that makes up the colour you want (*eg* cyan, magenta, yellow and black) is printed separately on film. These are known as separations and when they are laid over each other they combine to make the desired colour.

Stripping in photographs

Today it is easy to include high quality images in your documents. You can load a picture from a Photo CD or scan it in either yourself or at a bureau. However, high quality photos in your documents can cause the size of the file to become very large.

If your document is a catalogue or brochure with a large number of photos, you may find it easier to use low resolution images to position the photos and let your commercial printer strip-in the high resolution photos. With this process all the photos in your document are removed before the separations are produced, leaving just a box for positioning. The printer then produces the separations for you and strips the pictures in place.

DPI

Dpi is the term used to measure the resolution of your printout as dots per inch. Every letter, number or picture is made up of small dots (known as pixels) and the greater the number of dots in an inch-long line, the sharper it appears.

9
Design Advice

This chapter is full of good advice about design techniques and will explain some of the principles that you should keep in mind while you are designing your documents.

CONSIDERATIONS BEFORE THE DESIGN PROCESS

When you are designing a document you need to know exactly what you are designing. Before you even begin to think about how it will look on the page think carefully about what you want to achieve.

What is your document for?

The nature of your document will determine the basic layout. Your document may be something that the reader is not motivated to read and must, therefore, be encouraged to read. In this case, use every trick you can to make the document look inviting, such as an eye-catching cover page, colours, friendly easy-to-read fonts and short paragraphs. A piece of fiction that the reader chooses to look at may be a leisurely read and therefore the design should not come between the reader and the content. Keep it simple and congenial.

Position and size your items on the page according to their importance. The most prominent items on the page should also be the most important. Be sure that the information is clear and that the purpose of the document cannot be misinterpreted.

If your document is an advertisement for your company, you may want to include a company logo or use a set of standard fonts that the company uses for all of their advertisements. If you are designing a newsletter for your club, you may want to make sure that you comply to a set of guidelines about how it should be laid out, making sure that the design is the same for every issue.

Who will read the document?

The intended audience for your document will affect not only the layout, but also the overall tone and style. Before you even turn on your computer and start creating your document, try to form a picture of who your reader is. Actually picture the individual and not just a faceless group. Consider the age, sex, social background and interests of your reader. All of these points may seem trivial, but by building an image of your readers before you start work you can tailor your document to fit them. For example, very young and older readers have considerably different needs. Trendy, fashionable terms will not suit an older audience, just as using longer or more complex vocabulary will not suit a very young audience. Very young and very old readers will probably need larger fonts, but for different reasons. Older readers may have bad eyesight and very young readers may find it difficult to read small text.

You may not think that the social and ethnic background of your reader will affect the document, but there are many hidden traps if you do not consider it carefully. If your document needs to be translated into another language, be careful that any examples or graphics used have the same meaning in the countries they will be going to. An English proverb will not necessarily have the same meaning when it is translated into another language. If the proverb is translated literally, it could cause confusion. Some words in British English can also have quite a different connotation in American English.

Perfecting your image

First impressions count. What goes through the readers' minds when they first look at your document will affect the way they perceive it. Think carefully about the fonts and pictures you use and the way you lay the document out on the page.

Think about the tone of your document, this will affect the language, fonts and layout you use. If your document is a serious or technical document, use a font that gives this impression and structure your layout in a neat and organised manner. If you are creating a light-hearted document, use fun fonts and pictures and a more relaxed design layout.

Many companies and clubs have a specific style for all their documentation, whether it is an advertisement, stationery or a newsletter. There may be a certain layout and fonts that you must use or a company logo that needs to be included. This will limit your choices for design, but will also give you a clearer focus for the document.

Creating your document

The desktop publishing package you use can sometimes be the deciding factor when you are considering how to design your document. If you only have a basic DTP package, you may not be able to reproduce some of your ideas. If this is the case you have two options: keep your designs as basic as possible or buy a different package. On the other hand, a powerful desktop publishing package can sometimes overwhelm you with the number of different designs you can create. The risk here is overloading your document with all the flamboyant effects your package can create. Stylish effects can be very exciting, but too many are only distracting.

If you find it difficult to think of a design, take a look at the designs you see around you every day. Decide what you do and do not like about the designs and think about how you can reproduce what you do like in your own documents.

Reproduction and distribution

Before you actually get down to creating your document, find out how it will be reproduced. Will it be printed by a professional printer or is it an internal document that can be photocopied and distributed? This will affect the number and type of colours you use and the type and size of paper.

Think about how your document will fit into an envelope if it is to be distributed by post. Will it need to be folded more than once? Will this make the document look untidy? Do you need larger envelopes or a smaller page size? Will the document be read by more than one reader or more than once? If so, the paper will need to be more sturdy.

This is one area of design that people tend to overlook as they do not realise the impact it can have on their documents. Before you can create your document you need to have a clear idea of what your finished document will be used for.

When is it needed?

Work out your timescale – you may find that you do not have the time to produce the document you would like. Consider what you feel to be the most important aspects and concentrate on getting them right before you go on to develop your document. Remember, with the power of desktop publishing, moving items around your document is as easy as clicking and dragging.

A long timescale can sometimes be just as difficult to work to as a tight deadline. You need to be motivated and organise your workload to make sure that the document is ready on time. It is easy to say that something is not needed for months, but when you are closer to the deadline you may find there is still a lot of work left to be done. It is much easier to have the document ready in plenty of time and make any last-minute changes at a later date.

What is the budget?

The budget for your document will affect the way you design and reproduce your document. If you are on a tight budget you will need to keep the number of pages to a minimum and the type of paper may not be as luxurious as you would like. Concentrate on maintaining the quality within the document to compensate for a possible lack of quality with the materials.

Printing in colour can work out much more expensive than standard black and white printing. If you really must have some colour, try to stick to one or two colours throughout to keep the costs down as much as possible. Talk to your printer about the costs of reproduction before you decide on anything.

DESIGN OPTIONS

There are a number of guidelines to follow when you are designing a desktop publishing document. If you stick to these, you will have a solid basis upon which to build your document.

Keep it simple

Try not to over-use text effects and design styles in an effort to impress your audience, keep it simple so that you do not lose the purpose of the document in an abundance of over-the-top designs.

Be consistent

Use your design layout and terminology consistently throughout your document. Changing between different terms for the same subject or different page layouts can be very confusing for the readers. The message you are attempting to put across may be lost because the readers have lost track of what you are trying to say. Repeat your design elements on each page, whether this is the fonts you use, the text alignment or any colours and borders.

Make it clear

Make your message clear. While fancy designs may look good on paper, they do not always add to the clarity of your document. If you have to use a technical or rarely used term, make sure that it is properly explained either in the text or in a separate glossary.

Less is more

Limit the number of items on your page to a maximum of perhaps five, depending on your page size. An item can be a paragraph of text or a picture, as long as it provides a focal point on the page. Too much information on the page can make the document difficult to digest and the information can be lost in the clutter.

Space the items out and make full use of white space. A large amount of white space around an item will make it easy for readers to pick it out. White space on the page also offers a rest for your eyes and can make the page look more appealing and easy to read.

PAGE LAYOUT

Almost any desktop publishing packages allow you to create a page setup that will apply to your whole document. You can apply it to all pages or have different right and left pages. Using the page setup you can determine the page size, margins and column guides. Creating a basic layout for your document will help you to position your text and pictures accurately and consistently.

The size of your margins and the number of column guides depend on the size of your page. The standard setup is to have one margin slightly wider than the other. This makes the page look less rigid.

Try not to fill the page too much. A page with too much text will discourage the readers and make it look as if reading it will be hard work. Make use of the white space on the page; an open and relaxed page layout is inviting. Plan all of this beforehand and decide how big you want your paragraphs and pictures to be.

When you are designing your page layout you may want to create a document background that you can use throughout your documents. This will give your documents consistency and make it easier for you to create them as the basis of each page is already decided. Put the items that you want on every page on the background, such as headers and footers, page numbers, pictures or logos. This can be created as a template for your document that you can save and use for all your related documents.

Every page in your document does not necessarily need to be identical. Very often documents have slightly different left and right pages. This can be for a number of reasons, such as to give the effect of a symmetrical double-page spread or to make sure that the page numbers are on the outer edge of the page. Many desktop publishing packages provide a number of ready-made templates that you can use as they are or adapt to suit your own needs.

Positioning the items on the page

When you are planning your page, remember to keep related items close to each other so that the reader is searching for neither a visual nor mental link. Keep unrelated items separate using white space or a rule, making it instantly clear to the reader that those items are not connected.

There are a number of ways to help you position your items on the page accurately. Most desktop publishing packages have an option which will display a grid on the page so you can see where you are positioning your items. You may also have a 'snap to grid' option which forces your items into position at the closet grid line. You can also use your rulers to make sure that you have put your item exactly where you want it.

Layout guides (column guides) are guidelines that you can set up on your pages to help you position your items. These layout guides can normally be determined from within your desktop publishing package to suit your document. The guides will appear on the page on screen to help you position your items but will not actually be printed.

Headers and footers

Headers and footers are text that appears at the top and bottom of a page and provide information about the document. This could be the name of the chapter, section heading, the author of the document or the document title. The page number is often included in the header or footer.

Most desktop publishing packages have an option that allows you to set up and create headers and footers for your documents. This can be done by typing the specific header or footer for the whole document or by having the desktop publishing package pick up text formatted in a specific style and using it as the header or footer.

TYPOGRAPHY

Typography refers not only to the fonts you use, but also to the size of the fonts and the alignment, leading, hyphenation and many other features of your text. The typography depends on the nature and tone of your document and its intended audience.

What is a font?

A font is a group of characters (alphabet, numbers and symbols) that share the same design and style. Fonts have a character of their own and each font conveys a different image. Choose a font that has the same image as the image you are trying to create, whether this is fun and light-hearted, serious or technical.

Each character in a font is broken down into various parts.

Serif fonts

Serif fonts – *eg* Times New Roman – have small 'kicks' – serifs – attached to the edges of each letter. These serifs act not only as decoration to make the font pleasing to the eye, but also guide the eye from one letter to the next. The vertical and horizontal strokes of a serif font are normally of different thickness. The serifs make a serif font very easy to read, and therefore ideal for large amounts of text, such as the body text of a document.

Serif   Sans serif

Sans serif fonts

Sans is French for 'without', meaning the sans serif fonts do not have the serif, *eg* Arial. Sans serif fonts have blunt edges and their vertical and horizontal strokes are normally the same width.

Sans serif fonts are best used for small amounts of text, such as headlines or notes, as the simplicity and clarity of these fonts adds impact to it. They are ideal for use in large sizes, especially when surrounded by large amounts of text.

Which fonts should I use?

As a general rule you should limit to two the number of fonts you use in each document. Too many different fonts on the page will distract the readers and make it difficult to follow the text. It is important that the body text of a document is easily readable and that the words are instantly recognisable, which is why serif fonts are more often used for body text. Avoid using more than one serif or sans serif font in the same document. Although you may have done it for a reason, to the readers it will look untidy and as if you have made a mistake.

If you are adding callouts or captions to a picture or diagram, the text should use the same font as either the body text or the headings. This keeps the page looking tidy and organised, making sure that the callout or caption text fits in with the document as a whole.

Experiment with your fonts to help you decide which ones you want to use. Take a block of text and apply different fonts to the body text and headlines, but remember that text can look very different on the screen to how it looks on the printed page. Different fonts at the same size can take up different amounts of space on the page, so if space is tight, choose a font that takes up little space.

Headings

Which font you use for your headings depends on the image you are trying to project. Very often a sans serif font is used for the headings and a serif font for the body text. Sans serif font headings stand out clearly from the body text, making the section breaks immediately obvious. For a more subtle effect use the same font as for the body text, but style it in a larger size, bold or italic so that it stands out on the page. The idea is to create a contrast between the body text and headings.

The size of your headings indicates their importance. Main headings should be the largest and perhaps in bold. As the importance of the headings decreases, so should the size and perhaps the bold style. In documents on a large page size the most important heading could be two to four times larger than the body text. On a smaller page size, make the dominant heading around 50 per cent larger than the body text. Experiment with the sizes to see what looks best on the page.

Paragraphs

For most documents it is best to keep your paragraphs short. This makes your documents easier to read and gives the reader a short break in between paragraphs. Also try to keep the length of your lines to an easily readable length. Long lines of text can be difficult to read as the readers lose their way and have to concentrate on following the line. A maximum of ten words in a line is about right. There are two ways of splitting paragraphs in your document:

A standard line space above the paragraph, but with an indented first line, creates a classic look and takes up less room.

For a more modern feel, have a slightly larger line space above the first line and no indent. This takes up more room, but adds white space to the page, giving it a more open impression.

Leading and spacing

Leading and spacing are the terms used to describe the space between lines of text, words and letters.

Leading

Leading is the white space between lines of text, measured in points (roughly 1/72 inch). Most desktop publishing packages have a default line spacing of approximately 20 per cent larger than the text size. Body text with a point size of 10 will have leading at 12 points (this is usually written as 10/12).

If you need to fit a lot of text into a small space or you have very short lines of text, you may want to reduce the leading. This will make the page appear darker and possibly more difficult to read. If lines are too close together it is difficult for the readers to find the next line of text.

Too much space between lines of text can also cause problems for readers trying to find the next line. A larger line spacing is useful if you have long lines of text as it makes it easier for the readers to move along the line. A page of text with an increased leading can look more inviting because it will appear more open.

You must be careful to reach a compromise between too little and too much leading. Too little space darkens the page and makes it difficult to read and too much space can make the lines look as if they do not belong together.

Word and letter spacing

The word spacing of your text should only be adjusted if you need to fit more words into a section or if you want to avoid many hyphenated words. As with any text spacing, avoid moving the text too close together as it will darken the page and make it difficult to distinguish between the words. Adjusting the space between letters is referred to as **kerning**. In some fonts certain letters can have a larger space between them and may need to be kerned together, *eg* capital T's and lower case o's.

To   To

You can also increase the space between letters and use this as a design feature, perhaps spreading a word across the page.

L   E   T   T   E   R

Alignment
The alignment of text is the way that your lines of text line up with each other. In general, you should stick to one type of text alignment in your document. Any changes in text alignment should be used for short pieces of text, such as headings, notes or comments in the margin. Do not vary the text alignment for the body text. There are four different types of text alignment:

Flushed left
Flushed left text (left-aligned) has the left-hand edge of each line aligned and the right-hand edge is left ragged. This is probably the most commonly used text alignment as the left-aligned edges give the reader a marker for the beginning of the line and the ragged right edge gives a marker to move on to the next line.

Aligning text to the left creates an informal and relaxed image for your text. It also means that each word is separated by the same amount of space and you can avoid hyphenation. The ragged right edge of the text also adds white space to the page and makes it appear more open and accessible to readers.

Justified
Justified text (left- and right-aligned) has both the left and right edges of the text aligned, making the text more rigid. When text is justified the words and letters are automatically spaced to make them fit properly, which can cause the text to look untidy. Most often the space between words is increased, which can sometimes cause rivers of white space to appear through the text.

You will often need to adjust the word or letter spacing of justified text to make it fit more neatly.

Flushed right

Flushed right text (right-aligned) has the right-hand edge of each line aligned and the left-hand edge is left ragged. It can slow down the reading process as it makes the beginning of the lines more difficult to find as they are not necessarily in the same place every time. For this reason, flushed right text should be used with discretion.

Flushed right text is most useful for a caption for a picture or diagram, or for short notes that you want the reader to pay special attention to.

Centred

Centred text has ragged left and right edges and can be very hard to read. Avoid using long sections of centred text, which are difficult to read because the reader has to search for the beginning of each line. Centred text is most useful for headlines or notes that need to stand out on the page and should only be used in short pieces.

Widows and orphans

A **widow** is a word or part of a word that is on a line on its own at the end of a paragraph. An **orphan** is the last line of a paragraph that appears as the first line of a new column or page (see Chapter 7).

The easiest way to counter this problem is by re-writing the sentence to make the words fit more neatly. You could also adjust the word and letter spacing, but this might make the text look untidy. If you really do not want to re-write the text, look at all the possibilities. Can you adjust the line length? Can you change the size of the text? Can you move a picture to make more space? Any of these methods may solve your problem, but be careful that any changes you make are still consistent with the style of the rest of your document.

Hyphenation

Hyphenation is used to split a word over a line of text, using a hyphen (-). This is most useful when you have justified text and do not want to alter the spacing of the words. Most desktop publishing packages offer automatic hyphenation, which will split words according to their syllables. You will often have the option of defining a **hyphenation zone**, where you specify the maximum distance between the last word in the line and the right margin.

Hyphenated words can be difficult to read because it makes the readers hold the first half of a word in their mind as they move on to the second half. This disrupts the flow of reading and can sometimes reduce the impact of your text.

Colour

Using colour in your documents does not necessarily mean coloured text or pictures, you can also use coloured paper. Colour should be used to add clarity to your document, not just for the sake of using it. Use coloured text with discretion, it is harder to read on the page as it provides a weaker contrast against white (assuming you are using white paper) than black text. Use colour in your text to create a different tone and feel for that section. You can also use colour in your document to signify different meanings and as a signal to the reader. If this is the case, do not use too many colours, as the readers may not remember what each colour signifies.

If you are thinking of using a large amount of colour or coloured paper in your document, think carefully about what that colour will say about you and your document. If you are designing a serious document about the latest developments in chemical research, pink paper or pictures will certainly not create the right image. For serious documents, stick to white paper and perhaps a more stark colour, such as blue or green as a contrast on the page.

The general rule for using colour is to use it sparingly. Not only because it is more expensive to print a highly coloured document, but because too much colour can be very distracting. Using colours and colour printing is explained in further detail in Chapter 8.

PICTURES

Use pictures in your documents to emphasise a point, add clarity or just to brighten it up. Your pictures should be relevant and chosen carefully to suit the tone and feel of the document. Pictures should always add something to the page, too many will only diminish the impact. In many desktop publishing packages you can add a drop shadow to your pictures, giving the impression of depth and a frame around them. When you are considering where to put your pictures on the page, try to position them so that they lead your eyes across the page. This gives the impression of flowing through the document.

There is a large range of pictures you can use in your documents and the type you use depends on the effect you want.

Line drawings

Line drawings are pictures that are built from a series of instructions, which tell the computer to draw lines and shapes to form the image. Most clipart images are line drawings as their quality tends to be higher than bitmaps. Most desktop publishing packages supply a selection of clipart images that you can use in your documents royalty-free.

Because the quality of line drawings is higher, you can resize them without affecting the quality of the image. Also the higher the resolution your printer has, the better the image will be printed. Common line drawing file types are CGM, WMF and EPS.

EPS (Encapsulated PostScript) files are very similar to line drawings, but they have additional information about the size and position of the image and often a low resolution screen image. If the EPS file does not have a screen image a blank box will appear on your screen where the picture should be. This will be printed correctly if you print it to a Postscript printer. If you do not print to a PostScript printer, either a box will be printed in place of the picture or the screen image will be printed.

Bitmaps

Bitmaps are images that are made up of tiny dots (bits) that are grouped together to form the picture. This method of forming the picture can take up a lot of disk space. Also bitmaps can be reduced quite neatly, but when they are enlarged they tend to have jagged and untidy edges. Common bitmap file types are BMP, PCX and TIF.

Photos

Photos give the impression of reality and can express feelings more easily that other picture types. Photographs to use in your documents can be found in several photo CD collections. You can also scan photos to use in your documents.

Scanned images

Use a scanner to turn any picture you might have into a computer graphic. Scanning an image involves the scanner reading the picture as dots and processing these dots to turn them into a bitmap that you can then use in your documents. Make sure that the original picture is of a high quality as the better the original picture, the better the scanned image will be.

The trick with scanning is to keep the file size as small as possible while still producing good results. A common failing is that people try to scan their picture to the highest resolution possible, making the file size very large and therefore the screen display and printing will take a long time. At most, scan your picture to the same resolution as your printer; this will make sure that you have the best printed results possible. You may even find that some pictures produce equally good scanned images at lower resolutions. The best way to discover this is by trial and error until you achieve the result you want.

Many DTP packages support TWAIN, which is a piece of technology that lets you scan an image directly into your desktop publishing program. If your package is not TWAIN-compatible, you will have to scan your image into another piece of software and then import it into your document.

Other decorative techniques

A well-drawn graph or a labelled diagram or table can often make a point more clearly than words. Most desktop publishing packages will have either a utility to help you create your own or the facility to import them from other programs.

Once you have the pictures in your document you can adapt them to suit your needs. This could involve cropping the picture, adding a border or even changing the colour. Depending on the software you are using you can make a number of changes to the original image. Using a piece of technology called OLE you can either link or embed a picture into your document. A linked picture means that if the picture is changed, the change will be made to that picture in every document it is used in. An embedded picture means that any change only affects the picture in that document. This can be very useful if the picture needs to be updated and is used in a large number of documents.

Fancy first letters or drop capitals can have a very dramatic appearance and add a dominant feature to your page. However, make sure that you do not use them too often on a page as they can be a little overpowering. Try to use them only at the beginning of a chapter or section.

Other decorative elements that you can add to the page include borders or artistic flourishes. Borders can draw attention to important areas, such as notes in the text. Depending on the style of border or flourish you use, they can also evoke feeling and add flair to the document.

ADDING EMPHASIS

Depending on the nature of your document, you may find that you need to add emphasis to a word, sentence or picture. There are so many ways of adding emphasis to your document; be careful that your document does not lose its impact. Any emphasis should not disrupt the flow of reading, but should add to the document rather than detract from it.

There are a number of ways to add emphasis, depending on the effect you want to create. The most obvious of these is to add contrast – if the majority of the items on the page are small, make the item you want to draw attention to large. Add a dominant visual element, such as a border.

Colour

An easy way to create emphasis in a document is to add some colour to make it stand out from the rest of the text, especially if the rest is in black and white. This does not necessarily have to mean the text or even the paper, but perhaps a company logo, the headers and footers or borders. Even just the lightest hint of colour can make your document stand out from others. As mentioned earlier in this chapter, choose your colour carefully and make sure it matches the tone of your document. If you want to use more than one colour, use contrasting colours for extra emphasis, rather than similar colours.

Text

As mentioned above, you can use a different colour to make certain words or phrases stand out from the rest, but if your budget means only black and white, there are still a number of other options.

Italic text adds a gentle emphasis to words that you want to stand out. Italics will not necessarily leap out at you from the page, but they are certainly noticeable when you are reading through the text.

Bold text adds a much stronger emphasis that will be noticeable at first glance, but too much bold on a page can make the page appear darker and also give the impression of dark pieces of text dotted all over the page. Bold text is best used for headings or large text.

Underlined text is difficult to read as it makes the distance between lines seem smaller and makes the page look very dark. The underscore can also obscure the text descenders. Avoid using underlined text for emphasis unless it is very widely spaced.

CAPITALS should only be used in very small doses, such as short headings, as they can be difficult to read. Where possible use SMALL

CAPS as these are less distracting, especially if you are using them within the body text.

"Quotation marks" are useful for emphasising book or magazines titles that you want to stand out from the rest of the text, but do not want to draw too much attention to.

Reversed text is useful for emphasising short pieces of text – a couple of words at the most. It can make the page seem very dark if you use it more than once or twice. You will achieve the best effect if you use a sans serif font in a large point size.

Reversed text

If you want to emphasise a section or phrase, set it off from the rest of the text. Indent it from the main paragraphs, add a border around it or put it in a shaded box – whichever suits your document. Even adding extra space above and below the text will make it stand out. Extra white space is an effective method of adding emphasis.

Shapes and borders

Most desktop publishing packages will allow you to add borders around text and type text into different shaped frames. This can make the text stand out on the page. Typing text into a shaped frame, such as a circle or diamond, can add a creative flair and draw attention to the text. However, only use this technique for short amounts of text, such as a sales pitch on an advertisement, because it can be very difficult to read. The style of border you use depends on the overall effect you are trying to create. A simple box around text will add a stark contrast to the page, but it will not create a dramatic contrast against the remainder of the text.

EXPERIMENT

The most effective way to learn how to design your documents is by trial and error. Play around with all the techniques and styles suggested here and take a good look at what your software can do. Once you have found a style you like, stick to it and make it your own. Remember, you can learn as much from your mistakes as from your successes.

Appendix:
Software Advice

LOW COST DTP PROGRAMS

There is a vast choice of desktop publishing software for those looking for economy as well as ease-of-use and effective document design. Some of the programs available are listed below.

GSP Pressworks 3.0
GSP, Meadow Lane, St Ives, Huntingdon, Cambridgeshire PE17 4LG, UK.
Tel: +44 (0)1480 496575, Fax: +44 (0)1480 460206. E-mail: cserv@gsoftp.demon.co.uk, Web site: www.gspltd.co.uk

Corel Print House 1.1
Corel Corpooration Limited, Europa House, 3rd Floor, Harcourt Street, Dublin 2, Ireland.
Tel: 353 1 478-2855, Fax: 353 1 295-7723, Web site: www.corel.com

Microsoft Publisher 97
Microsoft Corporation, 1 Microsoft Way, Redmond, WA 98052-6399, USA.
Tel: 800-426-9400; 206-882-8080, Fax: 206-936-7329, Web site: www.microsoft.com

The Print Shop PressWriter 1.0
Broderbund Software, 500 Redwood Blvd, PO Box 6121, Novato, CA 94948-6121, USA.

Printmaster Gold Deluxe 3.0
Mindscape, 88 Rowland Way, Novato 94945, USA.
Tel: 800-234-3088, 415-897-9900, Fax: 415-897-2747, Web site: www.mindscape.com

Serif PagePlus 4, Professional Edition
Serif (Europe) Limited, PO Box 15, Nottingham, NG7 2DA, UK.
Tel: +44 (0)115 942 1502, Fax: +44 (0)115 970 1022, E-mail:
serif@serif.com, Web site: www.serif.com

PROFESSIONAL DTP PROGRAMS

For those users who are experienced in desktop publishing design,
there is a range of professional desktop publishing packages
available.

Adobe PageMaker 6.5
Adobe Systems, 345 Park Ave, San Jose, CA 95110-2704, USA.
Tel: 408-536-6000, Fax: 408-537-6000, Web site: www.adobe.com

Adobe Framemaker 5
Adobe Systems, 345 Park Ave, San Jose, CA 95110-2704, USA.
Tel: 408-536-6000, Fax: 408-537-6000, Web site: www.adobe.com

Corel Ventura 7.0
Corel Corporation Limited, Europa House, 3rd Floor, Harcourt
Street, Dublin 2, Ireland.
Tel: 335 1 478-2855, Fax: 353 1 295-7723, Web site: www.corel.com

QuarkXPress
Quark, 1800 Grant Street, Denver, CO 80203, USA.
Tel: 303-894-8888, Fax: 303-894-3399, Web site: www.quark.com

Glossary

Alignment. The position of lines of text relative to the margin and each other.

Ascender. The part of a lower-case letter that extends above the x-height, *eg* the vertical line of b.

Baseline. An imaginary line on which letters sit.

Body text. The main text of a document.

Bold. A heavier version of a font, *eg* **bold**.

Border. A frame that surrounds an item, group of items or the whole page.

Bullet. A symbol that precedes each item in a list, normally a dot •.

Callout. A label that identifies part of an illustration, diagram or picture.

Caption. A short sentence that explains a picture or diagram.

Centred text. Lines of text that are aligned to the vertical centre of each other and the paragraph.

Character. A letter or symbol from a font's character set.

Clipart. Pictures that are often included with software or can be bought on disks and used in documents royalty-free.

CMYK. The process colours of printing: Cyan, Magenta, Yellow and Black. The combinations of these four colours make up almost all the colours you could need.

Colour separations. The process of separating colours into their process colours (CMYK).

Column guides. Non-printing guides that appear on your page to help you position the items.

Crop. To trim a picture so that only the area you want is shown.

Crop marks. Marks that are printed on the page to indicate where the printed page should be trimmed to.

Descender. The part of a lower-case letter that descends below the baseline, *eg* the tail of y.

Drop cap. An enlarged first letter that drops below the first line of the text. Sometimes called fancy first letters.

Font. Commonly used to mean the collection of characters (letters, numbers and symbols) that have the same style.

Footer. Text that appears in the bottom margin on the page, *eg* page numbers, chapter titles, *etc.*

Grid. Lines on the page that you can use to help you position your items; the grid is not printed with the document.

Gutter. The extra space between the inner margin and the edge of the page to allow binding.

Hairline. A measurement for very thin lines, less than 1 point.

Halftone. The representation of a continuous tone picture, such as photographs, as tiny dots.

Header. Text that appears in the top margin on the page, *eg* page number, document title, chapter heading, *etc.*

Hyphenation. Splitting a word at the end of a line according to its syllables. The word is split by a hyphen.

Indent. The space inserted at the beginning of a line.

Italic. The sloped version of a font, *eg italic.*

Justified text. Lines of text that are aligned to both the left and right margins so that neither edge is ragged.

Kerning. Increasing or reducing the space between characters.

Landscape. The orientation of the page when its width is greater than its height.

Layout. The arrangement of items on the page.

Leaders. Dotted or dashed lines that lead the eye from one piece of text to the next.

Leading. The distance between lines of text, measured in points.

Left-aligned text. Lines of text that are aligned to the left margin and have a ragged right edge.

Letter spacing. The amount of space between letters.

Margin. The area between the edge of the paragraphs and the edge of the page.

Orphan. The last word(s) of the previous paragraph that appear at the top of the next column or page.

Pantone. A well known colour model in which colours are specified from a standard reference set.

Point. The standard measurement for the size of text: 1/72 inch.

Point size. The size of text measured in points.

Portrait. The orientation of the page when its height is greater than its width.

Pull quote. A short sentence or phrase that has been copied from the main body text and highlighted in some way.

Reversed text. White text typed on a dark background.

Right-aligned text. Lines of text that are aligned to the right margin and have a ragged left edge.

Rule. A straight line that is used to separate items on the page.

Runaround text. Text that wraps itself around a picture.

Sans serif font. A text style that does not have serifs (kicks) on the character, *eg* Arial.

Scanning. Using a piece of hardware that interprets a picture as a computer graphic.

Screen. The number of lines per inch of each colour that makes up a halftone image.

Screen angles. The angle assigned to process colours so that they do not make an undesirable pattern when they are printed.

Serif font. A text style that has serifs (kicks) on the end of each character, *eg* Times New Roman.

Small caps. Upper-case letters that are smaller than standard capitals and similar in size to the lower-case x-height of the font.

Template. An outline for your documents that has been created with the appropriate layout, text styles and any other aspects of your documents that you will need every time, such as a masthead for a newsletter.

Trapping. A process in printing when one colour overprints another at its edge, so that if the colours are slightly misaligned during printing, white gaps will not be left.

Widow. The last word of a paragraph that appears on a line by itself.

White rivers. White spaces that appear to run vertically through justified text, like a river.

White space. The blank space on the page.

Word spacing. The space between words.

X-height. the height of the main body of a lower-case letter, not including the ascenders and descenders.

Further Reading

DESIGN ADVICE

Basic Typography: A Design Manual, James Craig (New York, Watson-Guptill, 1990).

Collier's Rules for Desktop Design and Typography, David Collier (Wokingham, Addison-Wesley, 1990).

The Complete Typographer: A Manual for Designing with Type, Christopher Perfect (Little, Brown, 1992).

Desktop Magic Electronic Publishing, Document Management and Workgroups, John M Wood (Van Nostrand, 1995).

Desktop Publishing Design, Ronnie Shishan and Don Wright (Microsoft Press, 1989).

The Desktop Style Guide, James Felici (Bantam, 1991).

Design for Desktop Publishing, John Miles (John Taylor Book Ventures, 1990).

Design Principles for Desktop Publishers, Tom Lichty (Scott, Foresman and Company, 1989).

Graphic Design for the Electronic Age (the Manual for the Traditional and Desktop Publishing, Jan V White (Xerox Press/Watson-Guptill, 1988).

Home-Based Newsletter Publishing: A Success Guide for Entrepreneurs, William J Bond (McGraw-Hill, 1992).

How to Do Leaflets, Newsletters and Newspapers, Nancy Brigham with Marcia Catalfio and Dick Cluster (PEP, 1992).

Introduction to Desktop Publishing: A Guide to Buying and Using a Desktop Publishing System, David Hewson.

Looking Good in Print: A Guide to Basic Design for Desktop Publishing, Roger C Parker (Ventana Press, 1990).

Making a Good Layout, Lori Siebert and Lisa Ballard (Cincinnati, North Light, 1990).

Newsletters from the Desktop: Designing Effective Publications with your Computer, Joe Grossman with David Doty (Ventana, 1994).

Publishing Your Own Specialist Magazine, Alan Greene (London, Kogan Page, 1990).

Tips on Type, Bill Gray (Lund Humphries, 1989).

Typefaces for Desktop Publishing: A User Guide, Alison Black (Architecture Design and Technology Press, 1990).

Typography for Desktop Publishers, Mark Hengesbaugh (Dow Jones-Irwin, 1991).

Typography for Desktop Publishers, Grant Shipcott (B T Batsford, 1994).

DESKTOP PUBLISHING PROGRAMS

PageMaker 6 for Windows, David Browne (Peachpit, 1996).

PagePlus DTP Companion, Ian Sinclair (Peachpit, 1993).

PagePlus in Easy Steps, Richard Hunt (Computer Step, 1996).

Using PageMaker5 for Windows, Sharyn Venit (Que, 1993).

Index

MANAGING YOUR FIRST COMPUTER
How to perform core tasks and go on to achieve proficiency

Carol Dolman and Marcus Saunders

Anyone new to the world of computers can expect to be baffled by the huge array of equipment, programs, books, and above all, the mind-boggling jargon that goes with the territory. How much do you need to know to use a computer effectively? This book will guide the first-time or inexperienced user simply and painlessly towards making use of all major applications in the shortest possible time. With clear illustrations and practical exercises, the reader will be using their computer effectively right from the start. Carol Dolman and Marcus Saunders are both qualified computer technicians who have worked with computers since 1979. They run their own computer business, servicing and installing computer systems, and specialise in instructing those new to computing.

144pp. illus. 1 85703 502 X. 2nd edition.

USING THE INTERNET
How to make the most of the information superhighway

Graham Jones

Soon, nearly everyone in the developed world will have access to the Internet. This book shows you how and where to begin. Unlike other books on the 'Net', this down-to-earth practical guide, now in its second edition, will really help you to get onto the Net and start exploring the new 'information superhighway'. Using case examples, it illustrates some of the many benefits the Internet can bring, and the personal, business or educational goals you can achieve. Graham Jones is a leading business consultant and writer. He is the author of *How to Manage Computers at Work* in this series, and has contributed to many computer magazines. He runs his own publishing business that depends on the Internet for up-to-date information.

128pp. illus. 1 85703 504 6. 3rd edition.

MANAGING YOUR PERSONAL FINANCES
How to achieve financial security and survive the shrinking welfare state

John Claxton

Life for most people has become increasingly troubled by financial worries, both at home and at work, whilst the once dependable welfare state is shrinking. Today's financial world is a veritable jungle full of predators after your money. This book, now revised and updated, will help you to prepare a strategy towards creating your own financial independence. Find out in simple language: how to avoid debt, how to prepare for possible incapacity or redundancy, and how to finance your retirement, including care in old age. Discover how to acquire new financial skills, increase your income, reduce outgoings, and prepare to survive in a more self-reliant world. John Claxton is a Chartered Management Accountant and Chartered Secretary. He teaches personal money management in adult education.

160pp. illus. 1 85703 471 6. 3rd edition.

CREATING A WEB SITE
How to build a web site in a weekend and keep it in good shape

Bruce Durie

Anyone can have a Web site and anyone can design one – you don't have to be a computer wizard. All you need is a standard multimedia PC, a modem, some basic software, a few good ideas, a design and some free time. Whether you want your own home page, a site for your school, club, church or group, small business or major company, this book will provide you with the know-how to create your own Web site quickly, using step-by-step instructions. Bruce Durie works in education and has written hundreds of articles for a variety of publications including *New Scientist*, plus books and plays. He has constructed a number of Web sites both for clients and for his own amusement.

144pp. illus. 1 85703 505 4. 2nd edition.

MAXIMISING YOUR MEMORY
How to train yourself to remember more

Peter Marshall

A powerful memory brings obvious advantages in educational, career and social terms. At school and college those certificates which provide a passport to a career depend heavily on what you can remember in the exam room. In the world of work, being able to recall details which slip the minds of colleagues will give you a competitive edge. In addition, one of the secrets of being popular with customers and friends is to remember their names and the little things which make them feel they matter to you. This book explains clearly how you can maximise your memory in order to achieve your academic, professional and personal goals. Peter Marshall is a member of the Applied Psychology Research Group of the University of London and works primarily on research into superior memory. He recently assisted with the production of Channel 4's *Amazing Memory Show*. He is also author of *How to Study and Learn* in this series.

128pp. illus. 1 85703 234 9.

MAKING A WEDDING SPEECH
How to prepare and present a memorable speech

John Bowden

At thousands of weddings each year, many people are called on to 'say a few words'. But what do you say? How do you find the right words which will go down really well with the assembled company? Written by an experienced and qualified public speaker, this entertaining book shows you how to put together a simple but effective speech well suited to the particular occasion. Whether you are the best man, bridegroom, father of the bride or other participant, it will guide you every step from great opening lines to apt quotations, anecdotes, tips on using humour, and even contains 50 short model speeches you can use or adapt to any occasion.

166pp. 1 85703 347 7. 3rd edition.

SETTING UP A LIMITED COMPANY
How to run your business as a director and shareholder

Robert Browning

Limited liability represents a responsibility to the general public and gives business dealings a public face. Directors, too, have onerous reponsibilities. This book has been written by Robert Browning, a chartered accountant formerly in public practice with many years' experience of small businesses. It sets out simply how to decide whether a company is right for you and, if so, how to go about it. Apart from a detailed explanation of how to form a company, it covers the filing of statutory information, the opening of bank accounts, taxation, wages and salaries, marketing, auditing and accountancy, and the use of computers.

136pp. illus. 1 85703 452 X. 2nd edition.

BUILDING SELF-ESTEEM
How to replace self-doubt with confidence and well-being

William Stewart

People who improve their self-esteem find that their lives take on new meaning as confidence grows and well-being is enhanced. This practical, self-help book reveals how the ravages of faulty beliefs about self can be reversed, enabling the reader to develop a firm belief in his or her attributes, accomplishments and abilities. Through a series of exercises and case studies it provides strategies for bulding self-esteem; it will help readers set clear goals and work steadily towards them. It is also a valuable handbook for those who work in healthcare and counselling. William Stewart is a freelance counsellor, supervisor and author. His background is in nursing, psychiatric social work, and student counselling and lecturing at a London college of nursing.

152pp. illus. 1 85703 251 9.